SELF LEARNING OF DATA SCIENCE FOR FREE

AJIT KUMAR ROY

[SKILL DEVELOPMENT FOR DATA SCIENCE JOBS]

Copyright: akroy@2016

Product Description

The amount of data currently generated by the various activities of the society has never been so big, and is being generated in an ever increasing speed. This trend is being seen by industries as a way of obtaining advantage over their competitors if one business is able to make sense of the information contained in the data reasonably quicker, it will be able to get more costumers, increase the revenue per customer, optimize its operation, and reduce its costs. Big Data analytics is still a challenging and time demanding task that requires expensive software, large computational infrastructure, and effort. Data is the new basis of competitive advantage. Enterprises that use data and sophisticated analytics turn insight into innovation, creating efficient new business processes, informing strategic decision making and outpacing their peers on a variety of fronts. Successful data scientists come from a number of different disciplines: biostatistics, econometrics, engineering, computer science, physics, applied mathematics, statistics, machine learning, and other interrelated disciplines. Experience of applying the scientific method to many disciplines and areas of research will prove fruitful in the field of data science. This book is a very basic introduction to data science. It is designed particularly for the beginners having the aptitude to learn and pursue careers in the emerging Data Science. The main emphasis of this book is to help students for thinking about the world in data science terms and learn taking advantage of free online web resources. While some elementary data science skills will be appraised, the emphasis is on skill development through self learning. Skills are a must for data science. Data science, as practiced today, arises out of the "big data / cloud computing" world and complexity science. This means data science is an advanced discipline, requiring proficiency in parallel processing, map-reduce, computing, petabyte-sized noSQL databases, machine learning, advanced statistics and complexity science. I believe that data science is as much about mindset as it is about the skillful use of tools. Thus I want the students early in their careers to start thinking holistically about data science and related tools and techniques. There are many concepts and skills that a practical data scientist needs to know besides the fundamental principles of data science. These skills and concepts will be discussed in order to take advantage of free online data Science tutorials, courses, boot camps, videos, blog posts, podcasts etc. This book 'Self Learning of Data Science for Free' is perfect for aspiring or current data scientists to learn from the best. It s a reference book packed full of strategies, suggestions and recipes to launch and grow your own data science career.

From the author

Data science is a set of fundamental principles that guide the extraction of knowledge from data. Data mining is the extraction of knowledge from data, via technologies that incorporate these principles. Data science involves principles, processes, and techniques for understanding phenomena via the automated analysis of data. Data science as a profession and as an academic discipline is new, having been born in the first decade of the 21st century. Data Science is a flourishing industry. Countries and companies around the world are continuously experiencing a rush in the amount of data collected. They are determined to hire experts who can work on their data and improve their lives. Such experts are known by many names. Most popular is 'Data Scientist'. Among others include Data Engineers, Data Architects and Statisticians etc. A data scientist is someone who is better at statistics than any software engineer and better at software engineering than any statistician. Data scientist's most basic, universal skill is the ability to write code. Data Scientist means a professional who uses scientific methods to liberate and create meaning from raw data. With vast amounts of data now available, companies in almost every industry are focused on exploiting data for competitive advantage. In the past, firms could employ teams of statisticians, modelers, and analysts to explore datasets manually, but the volume and variety of data have far outstripped the capacity of manual analysis. At the same time, computers have become far more powerful, networking has become ubiquitous, and algorithms have been developed that can connect datasets to enable broader and deeper analyses than previously possible. The convergence of these phenomena has given rise to the increasingly widespread business application of data science principles and data-mining techniques. Big data technologies such as Pig, Hive, NoSQL dialect, and Map Reduce, Hadoop, HBase, and MongoDB have received considerable media attention recently. *Big data essentially means datasets that are too large for traditional data processing systems, and therefore require new processing technologies. As with the traditional technologies, big data technologies are used for many tasks, including data engineering. Occasionally, big data technologies are actually used for implementing data mining techniques. One of the most frequent questions we hear is "how do I become data scientist? Probably rising costs, changing demand, and the Internet are disrupting this traditional path and providing viable alternatives of self-learning through Massive Open On line Courses (MOOCs) that facilitates access to courses at an extremely low cost often free. Further Boot camps offer students a structured learning environment at a far more affordable rate compared with obtaining a Master's Degree. Therefore, felt the need to compile a book 'Self Learning of Data Science for Free' containing web addresses, links, tutorials, video, blog posts that will guide one to the right direction to become a Data Scientist for free. I am thankful to the LinkedIn & Twitter data science community, for exposing me to a many new concepts, and enriching me to write a book for future Data Scientists enabling skill development to grab the hottest jobs of 21st century.*

Contents

1.   The Road to Data Science

A lot of people ask me: **how do I become a data scientist?** I think the short answer is: as with any technical role, it isn't necessarily easy or quick, but if you're smart, committed and willing to invest in learning and experimentation, then of course you can do it. Data Science is a hybrid role that combines the "applied scientist" with the "data engineer". Many developers, statisticians, analysts and IT professionals have some partial background and are looking to make the transition into data science. And so, how does one go about that? Your approach will likely depend on your previous experience. Here are some perspectives below from developers to business analysts.

Java Developers

If you're a Java developer, you are familiar with software engineering principles and thrive on crafting software systems that perform complex tasks. Data science is all about building "data products", essentially software systems that are based on data and algorithms.

A good first step is to understand the various algorithms in machine learning: which algorithms exist, which problems they solve and how they are implemented. It is also useful to learn how to use a modelling tool like R or Matlab. Libraries like WEKA, Vowpal Wabbit, and OpenNLP provide well-tested implementations of many common algorithms. If you're not already familiar with Hadoop — learning map-reduce, Pig and Hive and Mahout will be valuable.

Python Developers

If you're a Python developer, you are familiar with software development and scripting, and may have already used some Python libraries that are often used in data science such as NumPy and SciPy.

Python has great support for data science applications, especially with libraries such as NumPy/Scipy, Pandas, Scikit-learn, IPython for exploratory analysis, and Matplotlib for visualizations.

To deal with large datasets, learn more about Hadoop and its integration with Python via streaming.

2.   Statisticians and applied scientists

If you're coming from a statistics or machine-learning background, its likely you've already been using tools like R, Matlab or SAS for years to perform regression analysis, clustering analysis, classification or similar machine learning tasks. R, Matlab and SAS are amazing tools for statistical analysis and visualization, with mature implementations for many machine learning algorithms.

However, these tools are typically used for data exploration and model development, and rarely used in isolation to build production-grade data products. In most cases, you need to mix-in various other software components in like Java or Python and integrate with data platforms like Hadoop, when building end-to-end data products. Naturally, becoming familiar with one or more modern programming languages such as Python or Java is your first step. I found it very helpful to work closely with experienced data engineers to better understand the mindset and tools they use to build production-quality data products.

Business analysts

If your background is SQL, you have been using data for many years already and understand full well how to use data to gain business insights. Using Hive, which gives you access to large datasets on Hadoop with familiar SQL primitives, is likely to be an easy first step for you into the world of big data.

Data science often entails developing data products that utilize machine learning and statistics at a level that SQL cannot describe well or implement efficiently. Therefore, the next important step towards data science is to understand these types of algorithms (such as recommendation engines, decision trees, NLP) at a deeper theoretical level, and become familiar with current implementations by tools such as Mahout, WEKA, or Python's Scikit-learn.

Hadoop developers

If you're a Hadoop developer, you already know the complexities of large datasets and cluster computing. You are probably also familiar with Pig, Hive, and HBase and experienced in Java.

A good first step is to gain deep understanding of machine learning and statistics, and how these algorithms can be implemented efficiently for large datasets. A good first place to look is Mahout which implements many of these algorithms over Hadoop.

Another area to look into is "data cleanup". Many algorithms assume a certain basic structure to the data before modelling begins. Unfortunately, in real life data is quite "dirty" and making it ready for modelling tends to take a large bulk of the work in data science. Hadoop is often a tool of choice for large-scale data cleanup and pre-processing, prior to modeling.

Final thoughts: The road to data science is not a walk in the park. You have to learn a lot of new disciplines, programming languages, and most important – gain real-world experience. This takes time, effort and a personal investment. But what you find at the end of the road is quite rewarding. There are many resources you might find useful: books, training, and presentations.

And one more thing: a great way to get started on real world problems is to participate in a data science competition hosted on Kaggle.com. (http://hortonworks.com/blog/how-to-get-started-in-data-science/)

Statistical analysis and data mining were the top skills that got people hired in 2014 based on LinkedIn analysis of 330 million LinkedIn member profiles. We live in an increasingly data driven world, and businesses are aggressively hiring experts in data storage, retrieval, and analysis. Across the globe, statistics and data analysis skills were highly valued. In the US, India, and France, those skills are in particularly high demand (**http://sumo.ly/a7vh via @reskillme**)

3.   How to Become a Data Scientist for Free

Everyone has a different style of learning. Hence, there are multiple ways to become a data scientist. You can learn from tutorials, blogs, books, hackathons, videos and what not! Many personally like self paced learning aided by help from a community it works best for many.

There are many <u>online courses</u> ***to consider, and new ones being created all the time:***

- Coursera's Data Science Specialization is 9 courses, plus a capstone project. There is a lot of overlap with General Assembly's course, and course quality varies, but you would definitely learn a lot of R.

- Coursera's Machine Learning is Andrew Ng's highly regarded course. It goes deeper into many topics we covered, and covers many topics we didn't. Keep in mind that it focuses only on machine learning (not the entire data science workflow), the programming assignments use MATLAB/Octave, and it requires some understanding of linear algebra. Browse these lecture notes (compiled by a student) for a preview of the course.

- Stanford's Statistical Learning also covers some topics that we did not. It focuses on teaching machine learning at a conceptual (rather than mathematical) level, when possible. The course may be offered again in 2016, but the real gem from the course is the book and videos (linked below).

- Caltech's Learning from Data teaches machine learning at a theoretical and conceptual level. The lectures and slides are excellent. The homework assignments are not interactive, and the course does not use a specific programming language.

- Udacity's Data Analyst Nanodegree looks promising, but I don't know anyone who has done it.

- Thinkful's Data Science in Python course may be a good way to practice our course material with guidance from an expert mentor.

- edX's Introduction to Computer Science and Programming Using Python is apparently an excellent course if you want to get better at programming in Python.

- CourseTalk is useful for reading reviews of online courses.
- Some additional courses are listed in the Bonus Resources section of the course repository.

Here is just a tiny selection of **books**:

- An Introduction to Statistical Learning with Applications in R is a favorite book on machine learning because of the thoughtful way in which the material is presented. The Statistical Learning course linked above uses it as the course textbook, and the related videos are available on YouTube.
- Elements of Statistical Learning is by the same authors. It covers a wider variety of topics, and in greater mathematical depth.
- Python for Data Analysis was written by the creator of Pandas, and is especially useful if you want to go deeper into Pandas and NumPy.
- Python Machine Learning is coming out in October 2015. The author, Sebastian Raschka, is an excellent writer and has a deep understanding of both machine learning and scikit-learn, so I expect it will be worth reading.
- There are an overwhelming number of data science **blogs and newsletters**. If you want to read just one site, Data Tau is the best aggregator. Data Elixir is the best newsletter, though the O'Reilly Data Newsletter and Python Weekly are also good. Other notable blogs include: no free hunch (Kaggle's blog), The Yhat blog (lots of Python and R content), Practical

Business Python (accessible Python content), Simply Statistics (a bit more academic), Fast ML (machine learning content), Win-Vector blog (great data science advice), Five Thirty Eight (data journalism), and Data School (my blog).

- If you prefer **podcasts**, I don't have any personal recommendations, though this list gives a nice summary of seven data science podcasts that the author recommends.
- Some notable data science **conferences** are KDD, Strata, PyCon, PyData, and SciPy. (You should also search for data-related **meet ups** in your local community!)
- If you want to go **full-time** with your data science education, read this guide to data science boot camps, and this other guide which also includes part-time and online programs. Or, check out this massive list of colleges and universities with data science-related degrees.

3.1 The Open Source Data Science Masters

I wrote myself a curriculum for learning Data Science with **freely-available resources**, which I open-sourced in The Open Source Data Science Masters. It's a free, community-owned resource.

The best way to keep up with others is to read interesting articles from top data science conferences. For example, have a look at these:

- http://www.ijcnn.org/
- XIII International Conference on Artificial Neural Networks
- International Conference on Neural Computation Theory and Applications

Sometimes you don't want to break your mind reading tedious scientific articles, so come over here regularly: Data Science Central it's fun and very useful, you can discover more resources yourself. There are already some amazing answers here for reading. If you are in for some listening, I found these **podcast feeds quite valuable** on the journey towards data science and also making commutes more interesting:

- Partially Derivative
- a16z
- Data Stories
- DataScience.LA Podcast
- Numbers and Narrative
- Podcast.init - Python and the people who make it great
- R Talk
- Talking Data Podcast
- The Data Skeptic Podcast
- The R-Podcast
- All Things Hadoop
- O'Reilly Data Show

I guess many people know about kaggle, The Home of Data Science, as the primary website to practice skills, try 101 competitions these are knowledge based.

If anyone interested in Machine Learning using ENCOG framework, please refer to this plural sight training Advanced Machine Learning with ENCOG.

The Open Source Data Science Masters has everything you need to know, from the Math to the programming.

It was actually written by someone who taught herself data science using all free / open source tools, guides, courses, etc, and became a Data Scientist at a neat start up in the bay area!

1. Focus on Computer Science, Statistics and their intersection. Also domain knowledge can't be stressed enough.

2. Use MOOC: Udacity Data Science Track, Coursera Data Science Track and some excellent courses such as Machine Learning by Andrew Ng.

3. Some great books: Element of Statistical Learning, Intro to Statistical Learning, Mining Massive Datasets, Python for Data Analysis, Programming Collective Intelligence, and many more.

4. After that, you should get your feet wet by competing in Kaggle. Start with the Titanic one, make sure that you fully comprehend the data set and the techniques processing the data before you move on to the next competition.

In addition to Coursera lectures, there are some on YouTube too:

Statistical aspect of data mining - Google course

Caltech - Learning from Data Machine Learning Course - CS 156

Stanford - CS 229 Machine Learning Stanford School of Engineering

University of British Columbia - lectures on Machine Learning undergraduate machine learning at UBC 2012Machine Learning 2013

University of Washington, Data Mining lectures http://courses.cs.washington.edu...

Udacity - Machine Learning course by Sebastian Thrun https://www.udacity.com/course/u...

<u>Web Data Mining</u>

<u>Rahul   Rai</u> mentioned   a   particular <u>Coursera</u> course,   but   I'd recommend you look at all the course offerings - in particular the 'Statistics,   Data   Analysis,   and   Scientific   Computing' here: <u>https://www.coursera.org/categor...</u>

3.2   Most Required Skills for a Data Scientist

Data scientist performs research and analysis on data and helps companies to improve business by predicting growth, trends and business insights based on huge amounts of data. Armed with data and analytical results, a top-tier data scientist will then communicate informed conclusions and recommendations across an organizations leadership structure. Successful big data scientists will be in high demand and will be able to earn very nice salaries. But in order to be successful, big data scientists need to have a wide range of skills that until now did not even fit into one department.

Learning how to become data scientist can be quite costly, with an average cost of $9,600 according to extension.harvard.edu. But if you know which skills employers are looking for you can find many free resources online. That is exactly what we did for you! Below are the required skills set for becoming a data scientist with top 3 free resources to learn each skill online.

Test your initial expertise level by taking our multiple answers test:

Here are the ***most required skills for a data scientist position*** based on ReSkill's analyses of thousands of job posts and free resources to learn each skill:

1. Python

Learn Python Programming from Scratch by Udemy Learn to program in Python by Code Cademy Learn Python.org interactive Python tutorial

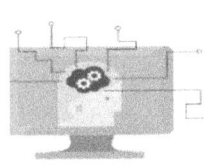

2. Machine Learning

Machine learning online Operational Intelligence and Machine Data with Splunk

3. R Language

R Basics – R Programming Language Introduction by Udemy Introduction to R at DataCamp Learn R at Code school

4. Big Data

Big Data University Big Data and Hadoop Essentials by Udemy Basic overview of Big Data Hadoop by- Udemy

5. Statistics

Statistics One by Coursera Statistics and Probability
Probability & Statistics

6. Data Mining

Data Mining and Web Scraping: How to Convert Sites into Data by Udemy Data Mining by Coursera

7. SQL

Interactive Online SQL Training for Beginners
Sachin Quickly Learns (SQL) – Structured Query
Language by Udemy SQL Tutorial by w3schools

8. Java

Learn Java: The Java Programming Tutorial for
Beginners by Udemy
Learn Java – Free Interactive Java Tutorial Learn
Java Programming From Scratch – Udemy

http://blog.reskill.me/how-to-become-data-scientist-for-free/ [1]

3.3   Free Online Resources for learning to Become Data Scientist

Learning how to become data scientist can be quite costly, with an average cost of $9,600 (according to <u>Harvard Extension School</u>). But if you know which skills employers are looking for you can find many *free resources online*. That is exactly what we did for you!

Below are the required skills set for becoming a data scientist with top 2-3 free resources to learn each skill online.

1. <u>Python</u>

<u>Learn Python Programming From Scratch by Udemy</u>
<u>Learn to program in Python by CodeCademy</u>
<u>LearnPython.org interactive Python tutorial</u>

2. <u>Machine Learning</u>

<u>Machine learning online</u>

Operational Intelligence and Machine Data with Splunk

3. R Language

R Basics – R Programming Language Introduction by Udemy
Introduction to R at DataCamp
Learn R at Code school

4. Big Data

Big Data University
Big Data and Hadoop Essentials by Udemy
Basic overview of Big Data Hadoopby- Udemy

5. Statistics

Statistics One by Coursera
Statistics and Probability
Probability & Statistics

6. Data Mining

Data Mining and Web Scraping: How to Convert Sites into Data by Udemy
Data Mining by Coursera

7. SQL

Interactive Online SQL Training for Beginners
Sachin Quickly Learns (SQL) – Structured Query Language by Udemy
SQL Tutorial by w3schools

8. Java

Learn Java: The Java Programming Tutorial For Beginners by Udemy

Learn Java – Free Interactive Java Tutorial

Learn Java Programming From Scratch – Udemy

For more information: **How to become data scientist for free and from scratch** [2]

AD Featured Online Program

Start your search with a respected online program that's recruiting data science students from around the US.

DataScience@SMU

Southern Methodist University's online Master of Science in Data Science program helps students develop the skills needed to manage, analyze and communicate findings from data to solve challenges. The flexibility of the online platform allows students to immediately apply the skills and strategies they learn through the interdisciplinary curriculum to their current jobs and graduate in 18–24 months. **GRE waivers available for experienced applicants.**

4. Self Learning of skill to become a good data Scientist

Data science is big landscape and self-learning is the necessary skill if anyone wants to become a good data scientist. MOOCs had been Major source of treasure for the data scientist. Though there are many sites offering MOOCs, but Coursera, Edx and Udacity have been leaders. Whether, your language is R, python, Java or C/C++ we have captured all of them. If, you are a beginner and understanding what data science is exactly or you are an expert looking for your next frontiers. You can search through this exhaustive list as per needed.

Some general guidelines about the source details:

- The level of the course is decided by considering the prerequisites, the efforts required and duration of the course.
- All courses assume basic background in the statistics.
- The courses are arranged with respect to level of expertise, i.e. beginners courses are listed ahead of expert level courses.
- The tools are considered as a programming language, or software tools used in the course.

4.1   The Analytics Edge (MIT)

Level:	Beginners-Expert
Effort:	10-15 hrs/week
Status:	Archived
Duration:	12 weeks
Prerequisite:	None
Tools:	R

This is one of the best courses to learn data science and analytics using R. The course provides in-depth lectures on multiple business cases, along with extensive exercises. Keep in mind, it is a very demanding course in terms of time commitment, but it is worth. The examples include Money ball, eHarmony, the Framingham Heart Study, Twitter, IBM Watson, and Netflix. Through these examples and many more, we will teach you the following analytic methods: linear regression, logistic regression, trees, text analytics, clustering, visualization, and optimization.

4.2   Machine Learning (Stanford University)

Level:	Beginners-Expert
Effort:	7-12 hrs/week
Status:	On-demand
Duration:	11weeks
Prerequisite:	Programming
Tools:	Octave

Whenever you will listen about the machine learning MOOCs, this course has to be there. Excellent course taught by one of the best professors in machine learning domain, Andrew Ng. The way complete course is well-organized and covers all core concepts of machine learning. Topics include: (i) Supervised learning (parametric/non-parametric algorithms, support vector machines, kernels, neural networks). (ii) Unsupervised learning (clustering, dimensionality reduction, recommender systems, deep learning). (iii) Best practices in machine learning (bias/variance theory; innovation process in machine learning and AI).

4.3   Data Science and Machine Learning Essentials (Microsoft) (24 Sep 2015 onwards)

Level:	Beginners-Intermediate
Effort:	3-4 hrs/week
Status:	Upcoming
Duration:	5 weeks
Prerequisite:	None
Tools:	R

Learn data science essentials with experts from M.I.T and the industry, partnering with Microsoft to help develop your career as a data scientist. By the end of this course, you will know how to build and derive insights from data science and machine learning models. You will learn key concepts in data acquisition, preparation, exploration and visualization along with examples on how to build a cloud data science solution using the Azure Machine Learning, R & Python. This course is organized into 5 weekly modules, each concluding with a quiz.

4.4 Databases (Stanford University)

Level:	Beginners
Effort:	8-10 hrs/week
Status:	Self-paced
Duration:	10 weeks
Prerequisite:	None
Tools:	SQL, XML query

If you are dealing with data, databases are inevitable. This course covers database design and the use of database management systems for applications. It includes extensive coverage of the relational model, relational algebra, and SQL. It also covers XML data, including DTDs and XML Schema for validation, and the query and transformation languages XPath, XQuery, and XSLT. The course includes database design in UML, and relational design principles based on dependencies and normal forms.

4.5 Coding the Matrix: Linear Algebra through Computer Science Applications (Brown University)

Level:	Beginner-Intermediate
Effort:	10-14 hrs/week

Status:	Archived
Duration:	10 weeks
Prerequisite:	None
Tools:	Python

Linear algebra is one the important building block of not only computer science, but also machine learning, graphics and statistics. This is a brilliant course guides you through the real examples and excellent python assignments. You will write programs to implement basic matrix and vector functionality and algorithms, and use these to process real-world data to achieve such tasks as: two-dimensional graphics transformations, face morphing, face detection, image transformations such as blurring and edge detection, image perspective removal, classification of tumours as malignant or benign, integer factorization, error-correcting codes, and secret-sharing. Another, more basic course is LAFF by The University of The Texas Austin.

4.6 Learning from Data (California Institute of Technology)

Level:	Intermediate-Expert
Effort:	10-14 hrs/week
Status:	Archived
Duration:	10 weeks
Prerequisite:	probability, matrices, calculus
Tools:	No restriction

It is one of the best MOOC ever for machine learning enthusiasts. This is an introductory course in machine learning (ML) that covers the basic **theory, algorithms, and applications**. But it requires one to have good linear algebra, calculus and probability background, along with coding skills. The course is taught by Yaser S. Abu-Mostafa, who is a Professor of Electrical Engineering and Computer Science at the California Institute of Technology. He is the co-author of Amazon's machine learning bestseller – 'Learning from Data' and great professor who simplifies the learning.

4.7   Data Science (Harvard Extension School)

Level:	Beginners-Expert
Effort:	7-12 hrs/week
Status:	Archived
Duration	16 weeks
Prerequisite:	None
Tools:	Python, d3

Excellent course, recommended to all the data science aspirants. This course introduces methods for five key facets of an investigation: data wrangling, cleaning, and sampling to get a suitable data set; data management to be able to access big data quickly and reliably; exploratory data analysis to generate hypotheses and intuition; prediction based on statistical methods such as regression and classification; and communication of results through visualization, stories, and interpretable summaries.

4.8   Introduction to Data Science (University of Washington)

Level:	Beginner-Intermediate
Effort:	10-14 hrs/week
Status:	Archived

Duration:	10 weeks
Prerequisite:	Programming
Tools:	Python, R, SQL

Introduce yourself to the basics of data science and leave armed with practical experience extracting value from big data. This course teaches the basic techniques of data science, including both SQL and NoSQL solutions for massive data management (e.g., MapReduce and contemporaries), algorithms for data mining (e.g., clustering and association rule mining), and basic statistical modelling (e.g., linear and non-linear regression).

4.9 Networks, Crowds and Markets (Cornell University)

Level:	Beginners-Expert
Effort:	4-8 hrs/week
Status:	Archived
Duration:	10 weeks
Prerequisite:	None
Tools:	None

The course examines the interconnectedness of modern life through an exploration of fundamental questions about how our social, economic, and technological worlds are connected. Students will explore game theory, the structure of the Internet, social contagion, the spread of social power and popularity, and information cascades. Another important source of knowledge for link analysis is SNAP.

4.10 Data Analysis: Take It to the MAX (DelftX) (1 Sep 2015 onwards)

Level:	Intermediate
Effort:	4-6 hrs/week
Status:	Upcoming
Duration:	8 weeks
Prerequisite:	Basic Spreadsheet exp.
Tools:	MS-Excel, python

Even in the era of the big data, there is a huge number of data analyst who rely heavily on the spreadsheets to gather the insights and its still relevant. This is an excellent course for those who want to enhance analytical skills using excel. You will take a deep dive into data analysis with spreadsheets: PivotTables, VLOOKUPS, Named ranges, what-if analyses, making great graphs – all those will be covered in the first weeks of the course. After that, you will investigate the quality of the spreadsheet model, and especially how to make sure your spreadsheet remains error-free and robust. Finally, you will also look into how Python, a programming language, can help us with analyzing and manipulating data in spreadsheets.

4.11 Text Mining and Analytics (University of Illinois at Urbana-Champaign)

Level:	Intermediate-Expert
Effort:	5-10hrs/week
Status:	Archived
Duration:	5 weeks
Prerequisite:	Programming

Tools: C++

This course will cover the **major techniques for mining and analyzing text data** to discover interesting patterns, extract useful knowledge, and support decision making, with an emphasis on statistical approaches that can be generally applied to arbitrary text data in any natural language with no or minimum human effort. You will learn the basic concepts, principles, and major algorithms in text mining and their potential applications.

4.12   Free Reference Material

The materials below are (legally) free, although they may require a little effort to find. I'm making it easy on you, and they are now all permanent residents of my digital library:

Open Intro Statistics 2nd Edition; Diez, Barr, Cetinkaya-Rundel – https://www.openintro.org (PDF)

R function reference cards – "cheat sheets" from a variety of authors – let me Google that for you

And some more advanced stuff …

An Introduction to Statistical Learning, with Applications in R; James, Witten, Hastie, Tibshirani – http://www-bcf.usc.edu/~gareth/ISL/ (PDF)

Elements of Statistical Learning, 2nd Edition; Hastie, Tibshirani, Friedman – http://statweb.stanford.edu/~tibs/ElemStatLearn/ (PDF)

Mining Massive Datasets, 2nd Edition; Leskovec, Rajaraman, Ullman – http://www.mmds.org (PDF)

5.   How to Become a Data Scientist for Free

Big Data, Data Sciences, and Predictive Analytics are the talk of the town and it doesn't matter which town you are referring to, it's everywhere, from the White House hiring DJ Patil as the first chief data scientist to the United Nations using predictive analytics to forecast bombings on schools. There are dozens of Start-ups springing out every month stretching human imagination of how the underlying technologies can be used to improve our lives and everything we do. Data science is in demand and its growth is on steroids. According to LinkedIn, "Statistical Analysis" and "Data Mining" are two top-most skills to get hired this year. Gartner says there are 4.4 million jobs for data scientists (and related titles) worldwide in 2015, 1.9 million in the US alone. One data science job creates another three non-IT jobs, so we are talking about some 13 million jobs altogether. The question is what YOU can do to secure a job and make your dreams come true, and how YOU can become someone that would qualify for these 4.4 million jobs worldwide.

There are at least 50 data science degree programs by universities worldwide offering diplomas in this discipline, it costs from 50,000 to 270,000 US$ and takes 1 to 4 years of your life. It might be a good option if you are looking to join college soon, and it has its own benefits over other programs in similar or not-to-so similar disciplines. I find these programs very expensive for the people from developing countries or working professionals to commit X years of their lives.

Then there are few very good summer programs, fellowships and boot camps that promise you to make a data scientists in very short span of time, some of them are free but almost impossible to get in, while other requires a PhD or advanced degree, and some would cost between

15,000 to 25,000 US\$ for 2 months or so. While these are very good options for recent Ph.D. graduates to gain some real industry experience, we have yet to see their quality and performance against a veteran industry analyst. Few of the ones that I really like are Data Incubator, Insight Fellowship, Metis Boot camp, Data Science for Social Goods and the famous Zipfian Academy programs.

Let me also mention few paid resources that I am a fan of before I tell you how to do all that for free. First one is the Explore Data Science program by Booz Allen, it costs 1,250 \$ but worth a single penny. Second one is recorded lectures by Tim Chartier on DVD, called Big Data: How Data Analytics is transforming the world, it costs 80 bucks and worth your investment. The next in the list are two courses by MIT, Tackling the Big Data Challenges, that costs 500\$ and provides you a very solid theoretical foundation on big data, and The Analytics Edge, that costs only 100 bucks and gives a superb introduction on how the analytics can be used to solve day-to-day business problems. If you can spare few hours a day then Udacity offers a perfect Nano degree for Data Analysts that costs 200\$/month can be completed in 6 months or so, they offer this in partnership with Face book, Zipfian Academy, and MongoDB. ThinkFul has a wonderful program for 500\$/month to connect you live with a mentor to guide you to become a data scientist.

Ok, so what one can do to become a data scientist if he/she cannot afford or get selected in the aforementioned competitive and expensive programs. What someone from a developing country can do to improve his/her chances of getting hired in this very important field or even try to use these advanced skills to improve their own surroundings, communities and countries.

6. Free Books, Videos, Blog Posts, Vodcasts, Twitter & Infografic Youtube, Amazon Web Services and free trainings to become a Data Scientist

1. **Understand Data**: Data is useless and can (and should) be misleading without the context. Data needs a story to tell a story. I have yet to find a "data scientist" who can talk to me about the "data" without mentioning technologies like Hadoop, NoSQL, Tableau or other sophisticated vendors and buzzwords. You need to have an intimate relationship with your data; you need to know it inside out. Asking someone else about anomalies in "your" data is equal to asking your wife how she gets pregnant.

2. **Understand Data Scientist**: Unfortunately, one of the most confused and misused word in data sciences filed is the "data scientist" itself. Someone relate it to a mystic oracle who would know everything under the sun, while others would reduce it down to statistical expert, for few its someone familiar with Hadoop and NoSQL, and for others it is someone who can perform A/B testing and can use so much mathematics and statistical terms that would be hard to understand in executive meetings. For some, it is visualization dashboards and for others it's a never ending ETL processes. For me, *a Data Scientist is someone who understands less about the science than the ones who creates it and little less about the data than the ones who*

25

generates it, but exactly knows how these two works together. A good data scientist is the one who knows what is available "outside the box" and who he needs to connect with, hire, or the technologies he needs to deploy to get the job done, one who can link business objectives with data marts, and who can simply connect the dots from business gains to human behaviours and from data generation to dollars spent.

3. Watch these 13 Ted Videos

4. Watch this video of Hans Rosling to understand the power of Visualisation..

5. Listen to weekly podcasts by Partially Derivative on Data Sciences and explore their Resources page

6. University of Washington's Intro to Data Science and Computing for data analysis will be a good start

7. Explore this GitHub Link and try to read as much as you can

8. Check out Measure for America to gain an understanding of how data can make a difference

9. Read the free book - Field Guide to Data Sciences

10. Religiously follow this infographic on how to become a data scientist

11. Read this blog to master your R skills

12. Read this blog to master your statistics skills

13. Read this wonderful practical intro to data sciences by Zipfian Academy

14. Try to complete this open source data science Masters program

15. Do this Machine Learning course at Coursera by the co-founder Andrew Ng of Coursera himself

16. By all means, complete this Data Science Specialization on Coursera, all nine courses, and the capstone

17. If you lack computer science background or want to go towards programming side of the data sciences, try to complete this Data Mining Specialization from the Coursera

18. Optional: depends on the industry you like to work with, you may want to check out these industry specific courses/links on data sciences, healthcare analytics – intro and specialization, education, performance optimization and general academic research

19. To understand the deployment side of data science applications, this cloud computing specialization from the Coursera and Youtube Amazon Web Services and free trainings are a must to do

20. Do these second-to-none courses on Mining Massive Datasets and Process Mining

21. This link will lead you to 27 best data mining books for free

22. Try to read Data Science Central once a day, articles like this can save you a lot of time and discussion in interviews

23. Try to compete in as many Kaggle competitions as you can

24. To put a cherry on the cake, these statistics driven courses will help you in differentiation from all other applicants – Inferential Statistics, Descriptive Statistics, Data Analysis and Statistics, Passion drive stats, and Making Sense of Data

25. Follow the following on Twitter for Predictive Analytics: @mgualtieri, @analyticbridge, @doug_laney,@ Hypatia_LeslieA, @hyounpark, @KDnuggets, and @anilbatra

26. Follow the following on Twitter for Big Data and Data Sciences: Alistair Croll, Alex Popescu, @rethinkdb, Amy Heineike, Anthony Goldbloom, Ben Lorica, @oreillymedia., Bill Hewitt, Carla Gentry CSPO, David Smith, David Feinleib, Derrick Harris, DJ Patil, Doug Laney - Edd Dumbill, Eric Kavanagh, Fern Halper, Gil Press, Gregory Piatetsky, Hilary Mason, Jake Porway, James Gingerich, James Kobielus, Jeff Hammerbacher, Jeff Kelly, Jim Harris, Justin Lovell, Kevin Weil, Krish Krishnan, Manish Bhatt, Merv Adrian, Michael Driscoll, Monica Rogati, Neil Raden, Paul Philp, Peter Skomoroch, Philip (Flip) Kromer, Philip Russom, Paul Zikopoulos, Russell Jurney, Sid Probstein, Stewart

Townsend, Todd   Lipcon, Troy   Sadkowsky, Vincent
Granville, William McKnight, Yves Mulkers

The whole list will take 3 to 12 months to complete and will cost you absolutely nothing, and I can guarantee you that with this skills set you really have to try very hard to remain jobless. Even if you complete half of it, send me a note and I will have something ready for you.

Ball is in your court, it doesn't matter where you are and how much you can afford, if you want to make at least four times higher the average income of your countrymen, this is the way to do it, at least for next 10 years (where we will be generating 20 TBs of data per year per person versus 1 TB of data per year per person in the last 10 years.) @ZeeshanUsmani

http://www.datasciencecentral.com/profiles/blogs/how-to-become-a-data-scientist-for-free [3]

7.   Videos for self learning

How Data Science is Preventing College Dropouts and Advancing Student Success

Educational institutions have a wealth of data around student demographics, admissions, academic per...Tags: Predictive Analytics, Big DataTim Matteson on Wednesday 216 views

DSC Webinar Series: From Visual Analysis to Presentation

While most of us understand how to analyze our data using visualization quite well, and well aware...Tags: Visualization, Data Story TellingTim Matteson Nov 10186 views

DSC Webinar Series: Data Analytics with Amazon Redshift: A Success Story

In today's latest DSC Webinar series you will learn how business intelligence and systems integrati...Tags: Sager Creek, Amazon RedshiftTim Matteson Oct 28255 views

DSC Webinar Series: Data Science Driven Approaches to Malware Detection

Malware detection within enterprise networks is a critical component of an effective information se...Tags: Anirudh Kondaveeti, Malware DetectionTim Matteson Oct 13210 views

DSC Webinar Series: Democratizing Data and Predictive Analytics While Ensuring Governance & Transparency

As organizations empower more users to fully leverage advanced and predictive analytics to "democra...Tags: Data Visualization, GovernanceTim Matteson Oct 7228 views

DSC Webinar Series: 100 Years of Data Visualization – It's Time to Stop Making the Same Mistakes

In 1914, New Yorker Willard Brinton wrote Graphic Methods for Presenting Facts, the first book on t...Tags: DSC, Big DataTim Matteson Oct 1294 views

DSC Webinar Series: 5 Things Your Organization Needs to Succeed in Data Science

What does it take to succeed in the world of Data Science and Analytics? It takes the right culture...Tags: Big Data, AnalyticsTim Matteson Sep 15279 views

DSC Webinar Series: When is the right time for real-time? Architectural best practices for Hadoop

Real-time processing is an important part of your Hadoop architecture, but is it always the best ap...Tags: Analytics, Big DataTim Matteson Aug 20138 views

DSC Webinar Series: How Do We Know That? An Introduction to Visualization Research

Pie charts are bad, right? Bar charts are good, but stacked bars aren't. And there are lots of the...Tags: Big Data, Robert KosaraTim Matteson Aug 4405 views

IoT: How Data Science-Driven Software is Eating the Connected World

The Internet of Things (IoT) will forever change the way businesses interact with consumers and eac...Tags: Predictive Analytics, Big DataTim Matteson Jul 21455 views

DSC Webinar Series: Faster Predictive Insight with Data Blending

Predictive analytics is only as good as the data you are working with. This can be a challenge in t...Tags: BI, Big DataTim Matteson Jul 8276 views

Deriving Analytic Insights from Machine Data and IoT Sensors

Hadoop and The Internet of Things has enabled data driven companies to leverage new data sources an...Tags: Predictive Analytics, Big DataTim Matteson Jun 25258 views

DSC Webinar Series: From Insight to Action – Predictive and Prescriptive Analytics from IBM

Predictive analytics has become an imperative for organizations as they strive to incorporate data-...Tags: BI, Big DataTim Matteson Jun 2336 views

DSC Webinar Series: 7 Reasons to combine SPSS Statistics and R

According to the Rexer survey,* R is the analytic software of choice for data scientists, business...Tags: Analytics, ModelingTim Matteson May 26336 views

DSC Webinar Series: The Beautiful Science of Data Visualization

Seeing and understanding data is richer than creating a collection of queries, dashboards, and work...Tags: Cognitive Science, Data VizTim Matteson Apr 28828 views

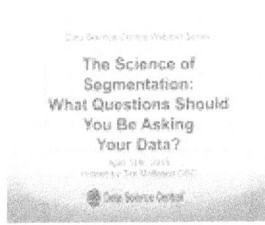

The Science of Segmentation: What Questions Should You Be Asking Your Data?

Enterprise companies starting the transformation into a data-driven organization often wonder wh...Tags: Predictive ModelsTim Matteson Apr 14744 views

DSC Webinar Series: Learn How To Work with Large Datasets to Build Predictive Models with Microsoft's Analytics Toolkit

In today's webinar we will use a case study of NY taxi data to discuss and cover how: • Azure provi...Tags: Big Data, Predictive ModelsTim Matteson Apr 1651 views

DSC Webinar Series: Data Lakes, Reservoirs, and Swamps: A Data Science and Engineering Perspective

In the fast paced and ever changing landscape of Hadoop based data lakes, there tends to be varying...Tags: Big Data, Data ScientistTim Matteson Mar 24450 views

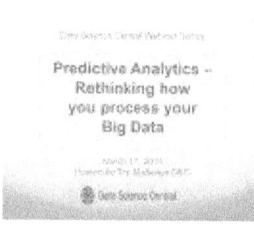

DSC Webinar Series: Predictive Analytics – Rethinking how you process your Big Data

Newer, Faster, Better…The tools that are coming to the Big Data market seem to reflect this quick d…Tags: Big Data, Data IntegrationTim Matteson **Mar 17810 views**

DSC Webinar Series: Better Risk Management with Apache Hadoop and RedHat

The risk management systems that each firm operates must respond not only to new reporting requirement … Tags: Analytics, HortonworksTim Matteson **Mar 3126 views**

http://www.datasciencecentral.com/video/video/listFeatured [4]

8. Free Resources for Machine Learning

Here you'll also find resources from the top universities teaching machine learning including cornell, MIT, harvard, carnegie universities. These are self-paced tutorials which includes slides, videos, blogs and what not! These resources are in no order.

1. Machine Learning course by Yaser Abu Mostafa – This is one of the highly recommended courses on Machine Learning. Usually, this course is provided on edX, but it has been closed now. It is expected to run again in 2017. You can still check out the course content and learn from them.

2. Machine Learning (Andrew Ng) on Coursera – This course requires no further introduction. If you are in data science, chances are you already know of this course. One of the best course on machine learning for beginners by Andrew Ng. It starts by covering linear regression and progresses towards higher level algorithms. This course is available for FREE!

3. Probabilistic Graphical Models – This course is provided by Stanford University on Coursera. The course instructor is Daphne Koller (co-founder of Coursera). This course teaches you the basics of PGM representation, methods of construction using machine learning techniques.

4. Neural Networks for Machine Learning – This course is provided by University of Toronto on Coursera. The course instructor is Geoffrey Hinton. This course will make you familiar with the applications of machine learning such as artificial intelligence, image recognition, speech recognition, human motion and how they are being used. In this course, Geoff has beautifully explained the basic algorithms & practical tricks to get machine learning working.

5. Scalable Machine Learning – This course is provided by University of California on edX. This course allows you to learn underlying statistical and algorithmic principles required to develop machine learning pipelines, implementation of scalable algorithms for fundamental statistical models, hands-on experience on Apache Spark.

6. Machine Learning Tutorials – Carnegie Mellon University – Carnegie Mellon University is widely known for its machine learning department. This resource provides tutorial videos & slides from the class of 2011. It consists of Andrew Moore's tutorials as well. This tutorial focuses on explaining the concepts of supervised, unsupervised and reinforcement learning by building models.

7. Machine Learning Quick Tutorials – Cornell University – Here's the course material of fall 2014 in Cornell University. This tutorial attempts to teach machine learning from the scratch using some interesting presentations. This course covers almost all the modules of machine learning. If you think you can't watch videos to learn these concepts, checking out these presentations should do well for you!

8. MIT Open Course on Machine Learning – This course is provided by Massachusetts Institute of Technology. If I am not wrong, this course has been archived but you can still access the course material. This tutorial aims to cover the underlying machine learning algorithms, starting from Regression, Classification till higher level concepts such as bayesian networks, collaborative filtering etc. It is available for download in PDF version.

9. Machine Learning Algorithms Tutorial by Andrew Moore – Andrew Moore is the Dean of the School of Computer Science at Carnegie Mellon University. Here are the set of tutorials which covers many aspects of statistical data mining, classical machine learning, foundation of probability to mention a few. These tutorials are available to download in PDF version. I'd highly recommended beginners to follow this tutorial.

10. CSCI E-181 Machine Learning – This course is provided by Harvard Extension School. It consists of video lectures which are focused on machine learning algorithm. Since, not everyone is fortunate enough to get into Harvard; you surely shouldn't miss the erudite discussions and knowledge being disseminated by Harvard professors in these tutorials. I really admired the pedagogy used by professors in these tutorials.

11. CSCI E-109 Data Science – This course is also provided by Harvard Extension School. I believe these are one of the best video tutorials available on learning data science in Python. The course instructor has beautifully explained such strenuous concepts using interesting examples and viewpoints. I'd recommend beginners to take this course as it covers every underlying aspect of data science and machine learning.

Some of the tutorials mentioned provide a high level overview of machine learning, hence if you wish to start from the scratch, you should start machine learning now.

http://www.analyticsvidhya.com/blog/2015/08/data-science-bootcamps-machine-learning-certifications/ [5]

9. TUTORIALS

General Introduction to Computer Science/Programming:

CS50: Edx Introduction to Computer Science

Think Python: Free textbook covering basic Python programming.

General Data Science

Data Analysis Learning Path: A Free Online Curriculum that provides a short but intensive introduction to Data Analysis and Data Science

Introduction to Data Science: Coursera course starting Jan 2014

Learn Data Science: Open content for self-directed learning in data science

SELF LEARNING OF DATA SCIENCE

The Open-Source Data Science Masters - Curriculum: The Curriculum for learning Data Science, Open Source and at your fingertips.

Introduction to Data Science: This book was developed for the Certificate of Data Science program at Syracuse University's School of Information Studies.

How to Prepare Data For Machine Learning: This blog post is a good primer on data preparation for analysis

The Analytics Edge: edX MITx course related to Analytics. With real-life examples and exercises using R.

Data Analysis And Statistical Inference : A online course on coursera giving a introduction to data science with programming assignments in R labs.

Think Stats: Free textbook that introduces basic exploratory data analysis in Python, linear and logistic regression, basic time series analysis and survival analysis.

Think Bayes: Free introduction to Bayesian statistics in Python.

Bayesian Methods for Hackers: An introduction to Bayesian methods and probabilistic programming with a computation / understanding-first, mathematics-second point of view. All is in pure Python.

R Tutorials

DataCamp: The Data Camp interactive learning platform is the fastest and easiest way to learn R programming and data science. Learn in the comfort of your own browser via tutorials and programming challenges.

R Tutorial for Beginners: A Quick Start-Up Kit: A really quick R tutorial

R Tutorial: R Tutorial from Clarkson University

Try R: Tutorial from Code School

swirl: swirl teaches you R programming and data science interactively, at your own pace, and right in the R console!

swirl online: There is now an online version of swirl as well. No installation or set-up required.

Check out a pre-compiled list of tutorials on R here.

If you want to learn about Excel for use in Kaggle Competitions, have a look here.

But what if you're a Pythonista? Well, then, you should click here then here to learn more.

Note that these tutorials or list of tutorials are found on the Titanic: Machine Learning from Disaster Competition Page.

https://www.kaggle.com/wiki/Tutorials [6]

10. Amazing and completely free resources online that you can use to teach yourself data science

Besides this page, I would highly recommend the Official Quora Data Science FAQ as your comprehensive guide to data science! It includes resources similar to this one, as well as advice on preparing for data science interviews. Additionally, follow the Quora Data Science topic if you haven't already to get updates on new questions and answers!

Fulfil your prerequisites: Before you begin, you need Multivariable Calculus, Linear Algebra, and Python. If your math background is up to multivariable calculus and linear algebra, you'll have enough background to understand almost all of the probability / statistics / machine learning for the job.

Multivariate Calculus: What are the best resources for mastering multivariable calculus?

Numerical Linear Algebra / Computational Linear Algebra / Matrix Algebra: Linear Algebra.

Multivariate calculus is useful for some parts of machine learning and a lot of probability. Linear / Matrix algebra is absolutely necessary for a lot of concepts in machine learning.

You also need some programming background to begin, preferably in Python. Most other things on this guide can be learned on the job (like random forests, pandas, A/B testing), but you can't get away without knowing how to program!

Python is the most important language for a data scientist to learn. To learn to code, more about Python, and why Python is so important, check out

- How do I learn to code?
- How do I learn Python?
- Why is Python a language of choice for data scientists?
- Is Python the most important programming language to learn for aspiring data scientists & data miners

If you're currently in school, **take statistics and computer science classes**. Check out what classes should I take if I want to become a data scientist?

11. Plug Yourself into the Community

Check out Meet up to find some that interest you! Attend an interesting talk, learn about data science live, and meet data scientists and other aspiration data scientists. Start reading data science blogs and following influential data scientists:

- What are the best blogs about data?
- What is your source of machine learning and data science news? Why?
- Data Science: what are some best users/agencies to follow on Twitter, Face book, G+, and LinkedIn?
- What are the best Twitter accounts about data?

12. Setup and Learn to use tools

Python

- Install Python, iPython, and related libraries (guide)
- How do I learn Python?

R

- Install R and RStudio (I would say that R is the second most important language. It's good to know both Python and R)
- Learn R with swirl

Sublime Text

- Install Sublime Text
- What's the best way to learn to use Sublime Text?

SQL

- How do I learn SQL? (You can practice it using the sqlite package in Python)

Learn Probability and Statistics

Be sure to go through a course that involves heavy application in R or Python. Knowing probability and statistics will only really be helpful if you can implement what you learn.

- **Python Application:** Think Stats (free pdf) (Python focus)
- **R Applications:** An Introduction to Statistical Learning (free pdf) (MOOC) (R focus)...   (more)

13.   Self Starter Way

For a self-starter novice, here is an outline that one can start with. (This is reproduced from blog- How to acquire the "Essential Skill Set"?- the Self Starter way).

Basic Pre-requisites:

- Mathematics, Algorithms & Databases: Mathispower4u-Calculus, Coursera-Linear   Algebra, Coursera-Analysis   of Algorithms, Coursera- Introduction to Databases

- Statistics: Probability   and   Statistics   for Programmers, Statistical Formulas For Programmers, Coursera- Data Analysis, Coursera- Statistics One

- **Programming:** Google Developers R Programming Lectures, Introduction to R - DataCamp, Scientific Python Lectures, How to Think Like a Computer Scientist

1. Acquire & Scrub Data:

- **DFS & Databases:** Hadoop Tutorial - Yahoo, AMP Camp Berkeley Spark Introduction & Exercises, Intro to Hadoop & MapReduce for Beginners - Udacity, BigDataUniversity: Big Data, All out beginner's guide to MongoDB

- **Data Munging:** Predictive Analytics: Data Preparation, Data Wrangling in Pandas, Analyzing and Manipulating Data with Pandas, Data Wrangler, OpenRefine

2. Filter & Mine data:

- **Data Analysis in R:** Data science in R, Coursera- Computing for Data Analysis in R

- **Data Analysis in Python (numpy, scipy, pandas, scikit):** Getting Started With Python For Data Science, Introduction to NumPy -SciPyConf 2015, Statistical Data Analysis in Python, Pandas (1st Video Below), SciPy 2013- Introduction to SciKit Learn Tutorial I & II (2nd & 3rd Video Below)

- **Exploratory Data Analysis-** Exploratory Data Analysis in R, Exploratory Data Analysis in Python, UC Berkeley: Descriptive Statistics, Basic Unix Shell Commands for the Data Scientist

- **Data Mining, Machine Learning:** Data Mining Map, Coursera - Machine Learning, Stanford - Statistical Learning, MITx: The Analytics Edge, STATS 202 Data Mining &

43

Analysis,Mining Massive Data Sets - Stanford, Learning From Data - CalTech,Coursera - Web Intelligence & Big Data

3. Represent & Refine Data:

Tableau-Training & Tutorials, Data visualisation in R with ggplot2 and plyr, Predictive Analytics: Overview and Data visualization, Flowing Data-Tutorials, UC Berkeley-Data Visualization, D3.js Tutorial

4. Domain Knowledge:

This skill is developed through experience working in an industry. Each dataset is different and comes with certain assumptions and industry knowledge. For example, a data analyst specializing in stock market data would need time to develop knowledge in analyzing transactional data for restaurants.

Combining all the above:

Data Literacy Course -- IAP

Coursera - Introduction to Data Science

Coursera - Data Science Specialization

Books:

Elements of Statistical Learning

Python Machine Learning

Apply the knowledge:

Harvard Data Science Course Homework

Kaggle: The Home of Data Science

Analyzing Big Data with Twitter

Analyzing Twitter Data with Apache Hadoop

14.   The Best Free Courses

My Slide Rule – Complete Learning Path: Data Analysis Learning Path by Claudia Gold- *(This prepares you enough)*

One of best all-in-one Box: The Open Source Data Science Masters

Extensive and Intensive **DSE Track**: Page on bitly.com *(In depth, complete mastery of every concept in analytics landscape)*

Fast Track on Data Tools: Page on coursera.org *(R, R Studio, Version Control, Real Projects)*

Roadmaps: Metacademy - Roadmaps *(Another awesome source)*

Sources by Components

Intensive Hadoop Specialization Hadoop Tutorial -- with HDFS, HBase, MapReduce, Oozie, Hive, and Pig (Right from installing until deploying Big Data apps) Hadoop Tutorial - YDN (Yahoo Tutorial) Page on cloudera.com (Fast Track Hadoop from Cloudera) Big Data University (A to Z free course of Big Data) Welcome to Apache™ Hadoop®! (From Hadoop itself)

For DB, Various Analytics, Machine Learning and other related Courses and Training on Analytics, Data Mining, and Data Science (exhaustive free list) DataTau (Latest Must Dos/Must Know from Analytics World) Page on www.hakkalabs.co (Data pipeline from Scratch) Machine Learning With R (ML with R)

Real World Problem Sets: Data Science: What are some good toy problems in data science? Find, Use and Share Numerical Data

Data Result Presentation and Data Visualization Tutorials \ Processing.org Tableau Public (**Tableau**) Big Data Analytics with Tableau Great tools for data visualization

Your Data Repository, Program and App Repository, and Result Portfolio Check-In Build software better, together

Real-World Competitions Competitions | Kaggle

15. Most Sought After Skills Employers Are Looking For Data Scientist Positions

Here are the most sought after skills employers are looking for Data Scientist positions, based on analysis performed on job postings (I also included some free resources I found for each skill):

1. Python

- Web Programming Beginners Course – Learn Python Programming
- Python
- Learn Python - Free Interactive Python Tutorial

2. Machine Learning

- Machine Learning on coursera

3. R

- Learn R Programming Language & RStudio Basics in 1 Hour

- R Programming Langauge - Code School
- Introduction to R | DataCamp

4. Big Data

- Big Data University
- Big Data and Hadoop Essentials - Udemy
- Basic overview of Big Data Hadoop - Udemy

5. Hadoop

- Big Data and Hadoop Essentials - Udemy
- Basic overview of Big Data Hadoop - Udemy
- Hadoop Training & Certification Course | Udemy

6. SQL

- Interactive Online SQL Training for Beginners
- Sachin Quickly Learns (SQL) - Structured Query Language
- SQL Tutorial

7. Statistics

- Statistics One on coursera
- Statistics and Probability
- Probability & Statistics

8. Java

- Learn Java: The Java Programming Tutorial For Beginners
- Learn Java - Free Interactive Java Tutorial
- Learn Java Programming From Scratch - Udemy

9. Data Mining

- Data Mining and Web Scraping: How to Convert Sites into Data

- Data Mining on coursera

A great way to acquire new skills and to grow your professional network is to attend meet ups: Data Science Meetups

You can learn more about the required skills to become a data scientist and get relevant resources here.

Statistical analysis and data mining were the top skills that got people hired in 2014 based on LinkedIn analysis of 330 million LinkedIn member profiles. We live in an increasingly data driven world, and businesses are aggressively hiring experts in data storage, retrieval, and analysis. Across the globe, statistics and data analysis skills were highly valued. In the US, India, and France, those skills are in particularly high demand.

16. Required skills set for becoming a data scientist with top 3 free resources to learn each skill online.

Here are the most required skills for a data scientist based on Re-Skill's analyses of thousands of job and free resources to learn each skill:

1. Python

Learn Python Programming From Scratch by Udemy
Learn to program in Python by CodeCademy
LearnPython.org interactive Python tutorial

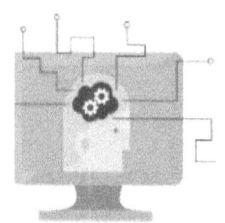

2. Machine Learning

Machine learning online
Operational Intelligence and Machine Data with Splunk

3. R Language

R Basics – R Programming Language Introduction by Udemy
Introduction to R at DataCamp
Learn R at Code school
Test your R skills

4. Big Data

Big Data University
Big Data and Hadoop Essentials by Udemy
Basic overview of Big Data Hadoopby- Udemy

5. Statistics

Statistics One by Coursera
Statistics and Probability
Probability & Statistics

6. Data Mining

Data Mining and Web Scraping: How to Convert Sites into Data by Udemy
Data Mining by Coursera

7. SQL

Interactive Online SQL Training for Beginners
Sachin Quickly Learns (SQL) – Structured Query Language by Udemy
SQL Tutorial by w3schools
Test your SQL skills

8. Java

Learn Java: The Java Programming Tutorial For Beginners by Udemy
Learn Java – Free Interactive Java Tutorial
Learn Java Programming From Scratch – Udemy

The Open-Source Data Science Masters

The open-source curriculum for learning Data Science, Foundational in both theory and technologies, the OSDSM breaks down the core competencies necessary to make data useful.

The Internet is Your Oyster

With Coursera, ebooks, Stack Overflow, and GitHub -- all free and open -- how can you afford not to take advantage of an open source education?

The Motivation

We need more Data Scientists.

...by 2018 the United States will experience a shortage of 190,000 skilled data scientists, and 1.5 million managers and analysts capable of reaping actionable insights from the big data deluge.

-- McKinsey Report Highlights the Impending Data Scientist Shortage 23 July 2013

There are little to no Data Scientists with 5 years experience, because the job simply did not exist.

-- David Hardtke How to Hire a Data Scientist 13 Nov 2012

An Academic Shortfall

Classic academic conduits aren't providing Data Scientists -- this talent gap will be closed differently.

Academic credentials are important but not necessary for high-quality data science. The core aptitudes – curiosity, intellectual agility, statistical fluency, research stamina, scientific rigor, skeptical nature – that distinguish the best data scientists are widely distributed throughout the population.

We're likely to see more non-credentialed, inexperienced individuals try their hands at data science, **bootstrapping their skills on the open-source ecosystem and using the diversity of modeling tools available.** Just as data-science platforms and tools are proliferating through the magic of open source, big data's data-scientist pool will as well.

And there's yet another trend that will alleviate any talent gap: the democratization of data science. While I agree wholeheartedly with Raden's statement that "the crème-de-la-crème of data scientists will fill roles in academia, technology vendors, Wall Street, research and government," I think he's understating the extent to which **autodidacts – the self-taught, non-credentialed, data-passionate people – will come to play a significant role in many organizations' data science initiatives.**

-- James Kobielus, Closing the Talent Gap 17 Jan 2013

17.   The Open Source Data Science Curriculum

Start here. Intro to Data Science UW / Coursera

- *Topics:* Python NLP on Twitter API, Distributed Computing Paradigm, MapReduce/Hadoop & Pig Script, SQL/NoSQL, Relational Algebra, Experiment design, Statistics, Graphs, Amazon EC2, Visualization.

Data Science / Harvard Video Archive & Course

- *Topics:* Data wrangling, data management, exploratory data analysis to generate hypotheses and intuition, prediction based on statistical methods such as regression and classification, communication of results through visualization, stories, and summaries.

Data Science with Open Source Tools Book $27

- *Topics:* Visualizing Data, Estimation, Models from Scaling Arguments, Arguments from Probability Models, What you Really Need to Know about Classical Statistics, Data Mining, Clustering, PCA, Map/Reduce, Predictive Analytics
- *Example Code in:* R, Python, Sage, C, Gnu Scientific Library

A Note about Direction

This is an introduction geared toward those with at least **a minimum understanding of programming**, and (perhaps obviously) an interest in the components of Data Science (like statistics and distributed computing). Out of personal preference and need for focus, I geared the original curriculum toward **Python tools and resources**. R resources can be found here.

Math

★ What are some good resources for learning about numerical analysis? / Quora

- **Linear Algebra & Programming**
  - Linear Algebra / Levandosky Stanford / Book $10
  - Linear Programming (Math 407) University of Washington / Course
- **Statistics**
  - Statistics I Princeton / Coursera
  - Stats in a Nutshell Book $29
  - Think Stats: Probability and Statistics for Programmers Digital & Book $25
  - Think Bayes Digital & Book $25
- **Differential Equations & Calculus**
  - Differential Equations in Data Science Python Tutorial
- **Problem Solving**
  - Problem-Solving Heuristics "How To Solve It" Polya / Book $10

Computing

Get your environment up and running with the Data Science Toolbox

- **Algorithms**
  - Algorithms Design & Analysis I Stanford / Coursera
  - Algorithm Design, Kleinberg & Tardos Book $125

- **Distributed Computing Paradigms**
  - *See Intro to Data Science UW / Lectures on MapReduce
  - Intro to Hadoop and MapReduce Cloudera / Udacity Course *includes select free excerpts of Hadoop: The Definitive Guide Book $29

- **Databases**
  - Introduction to Databases Stanford / Online Course
  - SQL School Mode Analytics / Tutorials
  - SQL Tutorials SQLZOO / Tutorials

- **Data Mining**
  - Mining Massive Data Sets / Stanford Coursera & Digital & Book $58
  - Mining The Social Web Book $30
  - Introduction to Information Retrieval / Stanford Digital & Book $56
  - *OSDSM Specialization: Web Scraping & Crawling*

- **Machine Learning**

Foundational & Theoretical

  - Machine Learning Ng Stanford / Coursera
  - A Course in Machine Learning UMD / Digital Book
  - The Elements of Statistical Learning / Stanford Digital & Book $80 & Study Group
  - Machine Learning Caltech / Edx

Practical

- o Programming Collective Intelligence Book $27
- o Machine Learning for Hackers ipynb / digital book
- o Intro to scikit-learn, SciPy2013 youtube tutorials

- **Probabilistic Modeling**

  - o Probabilistic Programming and Bayesian Methods for Hackers Github / Tutorials
  - o Probabalistic Graphical Models Stanford / Coursera

- **Deep Learning (Neural Networks)**

  - o Neural Networks Andrej Karpathy / Python Walkthrough
  - o Neural Networks U Toronto / Coursera

- **Social Network & Graph Analysis**

  - o Social and Economic Networks: Models and Analysis / Stanford / Coursera
  - o Social Network Analysis for Startups Book $22

- **Natural Language Processing**

  - o From Languages to Information / Stanford CS147 Materials
  - o NLP with Python (NLTK library) Digital, Book $36

- **Analysis**

  - o Python for Data Analysis Book $24
  - o Big Data Analysis with Twitter UC Berkeley / Lectures
  - o Exploratory Data Analysis Tukey / Book $81

Data Design

- **Visualization**

Foundational Information Design Books

- o Envisioning Information Tufte / Book $36
- o The Visual Display of Quantitative Information Tufte / Book $27

Theoretical Courses / Design & Visualization

- o Data Visualization University of Washington / Slides & Resources
- o Berkeley's Viz Class UC Berkeley / Course Docs
- o Rice University's Data Viz class Rice University / Slides

Practical Visualization Resources

- o D3 Library / Scott Murray Blog / Tutorials
- o Interactive Data Visualization for the Web / Scott Murray Online Book & Book $26

OSDSM Specialization: Data Journalism

Python (Learning)

- o Learn Python the Hard Way Digital & Book $23
- o Python Class / Google
- o Think Python Digital & Book $34
- o Introduction to Computer Science and Programming MIT OpenCourseWare / Lectures

Python (Libraries)

- o Installing Basic Packages Python, virtualenv, NumPy, SciPy, matplotlib and IPython & Using Python Scientifically
- o Command Line Install Script for Scientific Python Packages
- o Pandas Cookbook (data structure library)

More Libraries can be found in related specializations

- **Data Structures & Analysis Packages**

  - o Flexible and powerful data analysis / manipulation library with labeled data structures objects, statistical functions, etc pandas & Tutorials Python for Data Analysis / Book

- **Machine Learning Packages**

  - o scikit-learn - Tools for Data Mining & Analysis

- **Networks Packages**

  - o networkx - Network Modeling & Viz

- **Statistical Packages**

  - o PyMC - Bayesian Inference & Markov Chain Monte Carlo sampling toolkit
  - o Statsmodels - Python module that allows users to explore data, estimate statistical models, and perform statistical tests
  - o PyMVPA - Multivariate Pattern Analysis in Python

- **Natural Language Processing & Understanding**
  - NLTK - Natural Language Toolkit
  - Gensim - Python library for topic modelling, document indexing and similarity retrieval with large corpora. Target audience is the natural language processing (NLP) and information retrieval (IR) community.

- **Live Data Packages**
  - twython - Python wrapper for the Twitter API

- **Visualization Packages**
  - matplotlib - well-integrated with analysis and data manipulation packages like numpy and pandas
  - Orange - Open source data visualization and analysis for novice and experts. Data mining through visual programming or Python scripting. Components for machine learning. Add-ons for bioinformatics and text mining

- **iPython Data Science Notebooks**
  - Data Science in IPython Notebooks (Linear Regression, Logistic Regression, Random Forests, K-Means Clustering)
  - A Gallery of Interesting IPython Notebooks - Pandas for Data Analysis

Datasets are now here

R resources are now here

Data Science as a Profession

- Doing Data Science: Straight Talk from the Frontline O'Reilly / Book $25

Capstone Project

- Capstone Analysis of Your Own Design; Quora's Idea Compendium
- Healthcare Twitter Analysis Coursolve & UW Data Science
- Analyze your LinkedIn Network Generate & Download Adjacency Matrix

Resources

- DataTau - The "Hacker News" of Data Science
- Metacademy - Search for a concept you want to learn
- Coursera - Online university courses
- Wolfram Alpha - The smart number and info cruncher
- Khan Academy - High quality, free learning videos
- Wikipedia - The free encyclopedia
- The Signal and The Noise - Nate Silver Pop-Sci Data Analysis $15
- Zipfian Academy's List of Resources
- A Software Engineer's Guide to Getting Started with Data Science
- Josh Wills - The Life of a Data Scientist / Video
- Data Scientist Interviews Metamarkets
- /r/Machine Learning Reddit

http://datasciencemasters.org/ [7]

18. 7 Steps for Learning Data Mining and Data Science

You can best learn data mining and data science by doing, so start analyzing data as soon as you can! However, don't forget to learn the theory, since you need a good statistical and machine learning foundation to understand what you are doing and to find real nuggets of value in the noise of Big Data.

Here are 7 steps for learning data mining and data science. Although they are numbered, you can do them in parallel or in a different order.

Languages:	Learn R, Python, and SQL
Tools:	Learn how to use data mining and visualization tools
Textbooks:	Read introductory textbooks to understand the fundamentals
Education:	watch webinars, take courses, and consider a certificate or a degree in data science
Data:	Check available data resources and find something there
Competitions:	Participate in data mining competitions

Interact with other data scientists, via social networks, groups, and meetings

Also, don't forget to subscribe to KDnuggets News bi-weekly email and follow @kdnuggets - voted Top Big Data Twitter - for latest news on Analytics, Big Data, Data Mining, and Data Science.

Here I use Data Mining and Data Science interchangeably - see my presentation Analytics Industry Overview, where I look at evolution and popularity of different terms like Statistics, Knowledge Discovery, Data Mining, Predictive Analytics, Data Science, and Big Data.

1. Learning Languages

Recent KDnuggets Poll found that the most popular languages for data mining are R, Python, and SQL.

There are many resources for each, for example

Free e-book on Data Science with R

Getting Started With Python For Data Science

Python for Data Analysis: Agile Tools for Real World Data

An indispensable Python : Data sourcing to Data science.

W3 Schools Learning SQL

2. Tools: Data Mining, Data Science, and Visualization Software

There are many data mining tools for different tasks, but it is best to learn using a data mining suite which supports the entire process of data analysis.

You can start with open source tools such as KNIME, RapidMiner, and Weka.

However, for many analytics jobs you need to know SAS, which is the leading commercial tool and widely used.

Other popular Analytics and Data Mining Software includes MATLAB, Stat Soft STATISTICA, Microsoft SQL Server, Tableau, IBM SPSS Modeler, and Rattle.

Visualization is an essential part of any data analysis - learn how to use Microsoft Excel (good for many simpler tasks), R graphics, (especiallyggplot2), and also Tableau - an excellent package for visualization. Other good visualization tools include TIBCO Spot fire and Miner3D.

3. Textbooks

There are many data mining and data science textbooks available, but you can check these

Data Mining and Analysis: Fundamental Concepts and Algorithms, free PDF download (draft), by Mohammed Zaki and Wagner Meira Jr.

Data Mining: Practical Machine Learning Tools and Techniques, by Ian Witten, Eibe Frank, and Mark Hall, from the authors of Weka, and using Weka extensively in examples.

The Elements of Statistical Learning, Data Mining, Inference, and Predictionm, by Trevor Hastie, Robert Tibshirani and Jerome Friedman - great introduction for mathematically oriented

LION book: Learning and Intelligent Optimization, by Roberto Battiti and Mauro Brunato, freely available on the web, chapter by chapter.

Mining of Massive Datasets Book, by A. Rajaraman, J. Ullman.

StatSoft Electronic Statistics Textbook™ (free), includes many data mining topics

4. Education: Webinars, Courses, Certificates, and Degrees

You can start by watching some of the many free webinars and webcasts on latest topics in Analytics, Big Data, Data Mining, and Data Science.

There are also many online courses, short and long, many of them free - see KDnuggets online education directory.

Check in particular these courses:

Machine Learning, at Coursera, taught by Andrew Ng

Learning from Data at edX, taught by Caltech professor Yaser Abu-Mostafa,

Open Online Course in Applied Data Science, from Syracuse iSchool

Data Mining with Weka, free online course.

Check also free online slides from my Data Mining Course, a semester-long introductory course in Data Mining.

Finally, consider getting Certificates in Data Mining, and Data Science or advanced degrees, such as MS in Data Science - see KDnuggets directory for Education in Analytics, Data Mining, and Data Science.

5. Data

You will need data to analyze - see KDnuggets directory of Datasets for Data Mining, including

Government, Federal, State, City, Local and public data sites and portals

Data APIs, Hubs, Marketplaces, Platforms, Portals, and Search Engines

Free Public Datasets

6. Competitions

Again, you will best learn by doing, so participate in Kaggle competitions - start with beginner competitions, such as Predicting Titanic Survival using Machine Learning

7. Interact: Meetings, Groups, and Social Networks

You can join many peer groups - see Top 30 LinkedIn Groups for Analytics, Big Data, Data Mining, and Data Science.

AnalyticBridge is an active community for Analytics and Data Science.

You can attend some of the many Meetings and Conferences on Analytics, Big Data, Data Mining, Data Science, & Knowledge Discovery.

Also, consider joining ACM SIGKDD, which organizes the annual KDD conference - the leading research conference in the field.

http://www.kdnuggets.com/2013/10/7-steps-learning-data-mining-data-science.html [8]

19.   Getting a Free Data Science Education

As the field of *Data Science* continues to heat up fast, there are an increasing number of options to gain an education in this area. Many traditional colleges and universities are beginning to offer data science degree programs. But the educational option that's exciting a lot of people is the MOOC (massive open online course) through sites such as Coursera, edX, Udacity and others. I've decided to put together a **pseudo data science degree program** below that includes only free MOOC offerings (there may be a charge for a certificate if you want one). You won't have an official degree if you go through all the course material, but you will acquire a lot of practical knowledge designed to retool yourself and gain employment in the field.

Lower-Division Courses

Data Science 101 – Statistics One
Data Science 102 – Computing for Data Analysis
Data Science 103 – Data Analysis
Data Science 104 – Introduction to Data Science

Upper-Division Courses

Data Science 201 – Machine Learning I
Data Science 202 – Machine Learning II
Data Science 203 – Neural Networks for Machine Learning

Graduate Courses

Data Science 301 – Learning from Data (Caltech course CS101)
Data Science 302 – Machine Learning III(MIT course 6.867)

Free Data Science Books

To go along with the coursework, there also are a number of excellent free books available:

Mining of Massive Datasets

Bayesian Reasoning and Machine learning (pdf)

Information Theory, Inference, and Learning Algorithms

Gaussian Processes for Machine learning (pdf)

The Elements of Statistical Learning

Introduction to Machine learning (pdf) Think Bayes (pdf)

As the interest in data science continues to grow, and as the shortage in talent becomes apparent, the timing is excellent to retool you and climb aboard the data science gravy train. If you know of any other good educational resources for data science and machine learning, please leave a note for all of us.

http://insidebigdata.com/2013/09/19/getting-free-data-science-education/ [9]

20. Top-10-Online-Data-Science-Courses

As more and more of life's day-to-day work and personal activities are being simplified by Big Data technologies, the need for data scientists has risen remarkably for the past several years. Companies around the world scamper desperately to grab people with data science skills, and are willing to shell out big bucks to keep these data-crazed workers in their payroll. Experts agree that data science is still in its fledgling state, it will become a pervasive force pretty soon. If you want to learn data science and become a data science expert, check out our reviews of the following courses!

1) Harvard Data Science Course

The course is a combination of various data science concepts such as machine learning, visualization, data mining, programming, data munging, etc. You will be using popular scientific Python libraries such as Numpy, Scipy, Scikit-learn and Pandas throughout the course. I suggest you to complete machine learning course on coursera before taking this course, as machine learning concepts such as PCA (dimensionality reduction), k-means and logistic regression are not covered in depth. But remember, you have to invest lot of time to complete this course; especially the home work exercises are very challenging.

If you are good at statistics and programming take this course. 2014 version of Harvard data science course is going on. You can access the lecture videos here.

Prerequisites:	Cs50 and Stat 100
Programming Language:	Python
Course Length:	4 months
Difficulty:	Very high
Taught By:	Hanspeter Pfister and Joe Blizsten
Reviews by others:	Vincent granvelli has written a detailed review about this course. What is it to take cs109 — on Quora Ms. Natalia has written a review about this course.

2) Analytics Edge

The course gives a good intro to R and also gives hands on experience with statistical modelling techniques. The course has real world examples of how analytics have been used to significantly improve a business or industry. The workload is high, but the lectures and problem sets are well organized and structured. If you're interested in learning some practical analytic methods that don't require a ton of math background to understand, this is the course for you.

Prerequisites:	Basic knowledge of mathematics

Programming Language:	R, Libre office/Excel
Course Length:	11 weeks
Difficulty:	High
Taught By:	Dimitris Bertsimas and Allison Kelly O'Hair
Reviews by others:	Course Talk.

3) Machine Learning Course on Coursera

Data science and machine learning are closely related. Apart from machine learning the course shows you how to handle high dimensional data (Pca), introduces to map reduce, bias vs. variance, learning curves, etc. The course is taught using Octave (alternative for matlab), there are set of videos that shows you how to use octave. It is better to have some knowledge of calculus before taking this course, so Consider taking MIT multivariable calculus course.

Prerequisites:	Basic linear algebra and Calculus
Programming Language:	Octave
Course Length:	11 weeks
Difficulty:	Low
Taught By:	Andrew Ng
Reviews by others:	Class Central Machine learning course Review
	Course Talk Machine learning course Review

4) Data Analyst Nano Degree Udacity

A Nano degree, provided by Udacity and AT&T, is an online certification that you can earn in 6-12 months (10-20 hours/week) for

$200/month. Udacity's Data Science track teaches R, Python, MongoDB and Hadoop. The courses cover both theory and practice of Data Science, and every course ends with a project that allows you to demonstrate what you learned. The projects can be the start of your portfolio of work to share with others, especially recruiters. The prerequisites are pretty high, you need a variety of skills before taking this course.

Prerequisites:	Descriptive statistics, Inferential statistics, data wrangling, R, machine learning, data visualization, data science basics, computer science basics.
Course Length:	12 months (10 hours/ week)
Difficulty:	Very high
Taught by:	Chen Hang Lee and Miriam Swords Kalk

5) Introduction to Computational Thinking And Data Science

The course provides a brief introduction to plotting, stochastic programs, probability and statistics, random walks, Monte Carlo simulations, modeling data, optimization problems, and clustering. Even if you have little programming experience you can learn a lot from this course. The course serves as a motivation for the beginners in Python and data science.

Prerequisites:	Introduction to computer science and python programming
Programming Language:	Python
Course Length:	9 weeks (12 hours/week)
Difficulty:	Intermediate

Taught by:	John Guttag, Eric Grimson, Ana Bell
Reviews about the course:	Mooctivity

6) Coursera Intro to Data Science Course

The class gives a broad introduction to various concepts of data science. The first programming exercise "Twitter Sentiment Analysis in Python" is challenging, and rest of the assignments requires less time commitment. Professor Bill Howe assumes that you know statistics, Python, and SQL; you really need to know them because the lectures are so poor. Before taking this course, go through Stanford's data base course, learn Python programming concepts from code academy, learn basic statistics, and basics of machine learning. Don't expect this course to introduce you to these concepts. Despite its shortcomings, the course explains a lot about relational databases, Map Reduce and No -SQL. The course is not intended for beginners.

Prerequisites:	Basics of Python, statistics, basic knowledge of databases.
Taught by:	Bill howe
Programming language:	Python and R
Length:	3 months
Difficulty:	Intermediate
Reviews about the course:	Course Talk and Quora

7) Johns Hopkinson Data Science Course

R programming, exploratory data analysis and cleaning data modules are really well taught and practical. The statistical inference and regression model structure modules are not well organized; they have too much material for someone new to it. Data scientist tool box module is a waste of time; you can see the reviews of this module here: data science tool box.

Project swirl is a fun way to learn R. Most time the professor just reads the slides without adding any additional information. Certain concepts are not clearly explained, so you will spend more time goggling and learning those concepts. It is too traditional and too heavy in statistics in particular.

Prerequisites: Working knowledge of mathematics up to algebra and some programming knowledge.

Taught by:	Brian Caffo
Programming language:	R
Length:	12 months
Difficulty:	Intermediate
Reviews about the course:	Tech Powered math

8) Foundations of Data Analysis

The course focuses only on statistics and gives hands on experience with descriptive and inferential statistical concepts in R. If you want to learn R and statistical concepts, then this course is for you. You will be working with well formatted data sets, so you won't be learning data munging in this course. At end of this course you will be comfortable using different statistical techniques to solve your own problems about your own data using R.

Prerequisites:	None
Taught by:	Micheal J. Mahometa
Programming language:	R
Length:	13 weeks (3-6 hours/week)

Difficulty:	Intermediate
Reviews about the course:	Course Talk

9) Data Science In Action

The course is based on the book *"Process Mining"* written by professor *Wil van der Aals.* If you are a business professional and don't have prior programming experience, then this course is for you. The course acts as a classical divide between "business" and "IT". The course uses many examples using real-life event logs to illustrate the concepts and algorithms. After taking this course, you will be able to run process mining projects and have a good understanding of the Business Process Intelligence field.

Prerequisites:	A basic understanding of logic, sets, and statistics (at the undergraduate level).
Taught by:	Wil Van Der Aalst
Programming Language/Tools:	ProM, Disco, Rapid Miner
Length:	13 weeks (3-6 hours/week)
Difficulty:	Easy

10) Mining Massive Datasets

The class will introduce you to fundamental algorithms and techniques to deal with Big Data, such as MapReduce, Locality Sensitive Hashing, Page Rank, and algorithms for Large Graphs and Data Streams. It will teach you how to apply these tool-kits to important practical applications, such as Web Search, Recommender Systems and Online Advertising. This course gives a special attention to dimensionality reduction. A book based on this course is available for free. The course expects you to have good knowledge of database and algorithms.

Prerequisites:	Basic course on algorithms, data structures and databases
Taught by:	Jure Leskovec, Anand Rajaraman, Jeff Ulman
Programming Language/Tools:	SQL
Length:	7 weeks
Difficulty:	Intermediate
Reviews about the course:	Quora

Some of the upcoming courses in data analysis are computational methods for data analysis, data analysis and statistical inference, coding the matrix. Data camp is a great place to learn R. To learn Python for data analysis, you can check out my post.

So, what other courses are worth taking if you want to get a good education in data science?

- See more at: http://bigdata-madesimple.com/review-of-top-10-online-data-science-courses/#sthash.aXkg57KM.dpuf

http://bigdata-madesimple.com/review-of-top-10-online-data-science-courses/ [(10)]

21. Software Engineering Podcasts for Data Science

If you are a former software engineer looking to gain some data science skills, here are a list of podcasts that will most likely interest you.

21.1   Software Engineering Daily

A nice podcast which just ran a series of podcasts about data science.

- Data Science Overview with Yad Faeq
- Applied Data Science with Edwin Chen
- Kaggle with Ben Hamner
- Teaching Data Science with Vik Paruchuri
- Bridging Data Science and Engineering with Greg Lamp from Yhat
- Replacing Hadoop with Joe Doliner
- Data and Mental Health with Daniel Tunkelang

21.2   Software Engineering Radio

Great software engineering podcast, here are a couple of topics related to data science. Enjoy some listening while you are on the train, plane, bus or car.

- Episode 222: Nathan Marz on Real-Time Processing with Apache Storm
- Episode 219: Apache Kafka with Jun Rao

22.   30 Simple Data Visualization Tools

Visual media are increasingly generated, manipulated, and transmitted by computers. When well designed, such displays capitalize on human facilities for processing visual information and thereby improve comprehension, memory, inference, and decision making. Yet the digital tools for transforming data into visualizations still require low-level interaction by skilled human designers. As a result, producing effective visualizations can take hours or days and consume considerable human effort. Data visualization is not just about making what you found look good – often it is a way of gaining insight into the data. We just understand graphical information on a better level than we understand numbers and tables. Need a simple tool to create a fantastic data visualization? Here are 30 different notable pieces of data visualization softwares good for any designer's repertoire.

1. iCharts

iCharts is a platform that connects the publishers of market research, economic and industry data with professional consumers. iCharts hosts tens of thousands of charts in business, economy, sports, and other categories. iChart makes it simple for people to discover and follow the world's latest data insights. iCharts provides cloud-based and patented charting tool that enable companies and individuals to brand, market, and share their data as chart content to millions of viewers across the web. iCharts provides free accounts to the users which let you create basic interactive charts, while you can buy the premium version as well with tons of features. Charts can have interactive elements, and can pull data from Google Docs, Excel spreadsheets, and other sources. [Link]

2. Fusion Charts Suit XT

Fusion Charts Suite XT is a professional and premium JavaScript chart library that enables us to create any type of chart. It uses SVG and has support for 90+ chart types, including 3-D, gantt, funnel, various gauges, and even maps of world/continents/countries/states. Also, most of the charts have both 2-D and 3-D versions. Charts are completely customizable. The labels, fonts, colors, borders, etc. can all be changed.

And, they are heavily interactive with tooltips, clickable legend keys, drill-down, zooming/scrolling, and one-click chart export or print. [Link]

3. Modest Maps

Modest Maps is a small, extensible, and free library for designers and developers who want to use interactive maps in their own projects. It provides a core set of features in a tight, clean package with plenty of hooks for additional functionality. [Link]

4. Pizza Pie Charts

Pizza Pie Charts is a responsive pie chart based on the Snap SVG framework from Adobe. It focuses on easy integration via HTML markup and CSS instead of JavaScript objects, although you can pass JavaScript objects to Pizza as well. You can deliver pie charts to any device with Pizza. Your pie will be steaming hot with SVG so that it looks good on retina devices and HiDPI devices. And the pie will fit the width of your box–um, container–or can be given a max-width or max-height. [Link]

5. Raw

Raw is a free and open-source web application for visualizing data flexibly and as easy as possible. It actually defines itself as "the missing link between spreadsheet applications and vector graphics editors." The application works by loading a dataset by copy-pasting or drag 'n' dropping and allows us to customize the view/hierarchy. Raw is based on the popular D3.js and supports lots of different chart types like bubble, tree map, circle packing, and more. Installing Raw is pretty straightforward as everything works client-side. [Link]

6. Leaflet

Leaflet is a modern open-source JavaScript library for mobile-friendly interactive maps. It is developed by Vladimir Agafonkin with a team of dedicated contributors. Weighing just about 31 KB of JS, it has all the features most developers ever need for online maps. Leaflet is designed with simplicity, performance, and usability in mind. It works efficiently across all major desktop and mobile platforms out of the box, taking advantage of HTML5 and CSS3 on modern browsers while still being accessible on older ones. [Link]

7. Chartkick

Chartkick is a Ruby gem (also has a JavaScript API which doesn't require Ruby) for creating good-looking charts very easily and quickly. It integrates with two charting libraries: High charts and Google Charts where it is possible to use the same functions for generating charts with each library. There is support for multiple chart types and multiple series in a single chart. And, like mentioned there is also Chartkick.js which brings the same functionality to the client-side, without Ruby. [Link]

8. Ember Charts

Ember Charts is a charting library built with the Ember.js and D3.js frameworks. It includes time series, bar, pie, and scatter charts which are easy to extend and modify. The out-of-the-box behavior these chart components represents their thoughts on best practices in chart interactivity and presentation. [Link]

9. Springy

Springy is a force-directed graph layout algorithm. It means that springy uses some real-world physics to try and figure out how to show a network graph in a way that looks good. Springy.js is designed to be small and simple. It provides an abstraction for graph manipulation and for calculating the layout and not too much else. The details of drawing and interaction are mostly up to you. This means you can use canvas, SVG, WebGL, or even just a plain old positioned HTML element. [Link]

10. Bonsai

Bonsai is an open-source JavaScript library for creating graphics and animations. The library renders the outputs using SVG and comes with an intuitive, feature-rich API. There is support for creating simple shapes (rectangle, circle, ellipse, etc.) with specific functions and a path function exists for drawing any custom shapes. It is possible to apply colors, gradients and filters (grayscale, blur, opacity and more) to these shapes. Many mouse (or touch) and keyboard events are already built-in to the library and they can be managed easily. [Link]

11. Google Charts

Google Charts provides a perfect way to visualize data on your website. From simple line charts to complex hierarchical tree maps, the chart gallery provides a large number of ready-to-use chart types. It's an especially useful tool for specialist visualizations such as geo charts and gauges, and it also includes built-in animation and user interaction controls. [Link]

12. jsDraw2DX

jsDraw2DX is a standalone JavaScript library for creating any type of interactive graphics with SVG (and VML for old IE browsers). Besides the ability to generate all basic shapes like line, rectangle, polygon, circle, ellipse, arc, etc., the library can draw curves, Beziers (any degree), function plots, images and decorated text. [Link]

13. Cube

Cube is an open-source system for visualizing time series data, built on MongoDB, Node, and D3. If you send Cube time stamped events (with optional structured data), you can easily build real-time visualizations of aggregate metrics for internal dashboards. For example, you might use Cube to monitor traffic to your website, counting the number of requests in five-minute intervals. [Link]

14. Gantti

Gantti is an open-source PHP class for generating Gantt charts on-the-fly. The charts created are pure HTML5-CSS3 with no JavaScript involved. The output looks very nice by default but can be customized with ease (with SASS style sheet). It simply works by defining an array of start/end dates and calling a single function. Also, charts are cross browser (IE7+). [Link]

15. Smoothie Charts

Smoothie Charts is a really small charting library designed for live streaming data. Joe Walnes wanted to show real-time streaming data pushed over a WebSocket. Although many of the charting libraries allow you to dynamically update data, none have really been optimized for a constant stream of data. Smoothie Charts only works on Chrome and Safari. And it doesn't support legends. Or pie-charts. In fact, it's inferior in virtually every way to a library like Flot. But, it's very good at displaying streaming data. [Link]

16. Envision.js

Envision.js is a JavaScript library to simplify creating fast and interactive HTML5 visualizations. It comes with two chart types; Time Series + Finance and with an API for developers to build custom charts. The library is built on top of Flotr2 and the HTML5 Canvas. It is framework agnostic and depends on few micro libraries. [Link]

79

17. BirdEye

BirdEye is the Declarative Visual Analytics Library. It is a community project to advance the design and development of a comprehensive open-source information visualization and visual analytics library for Adobe Flex. The action script-based library enables users to create multi-dimensional data visualization interfaces for the analysis and presentation of information. [Link]

18. Arbor.js

Arbor.js is a graph visualization library built with web workers and jQuery. It provides an efficient, force-directed layout algorithm, abstractions for graph organization and screen refresh handling. The library doesn't force a specific method for screen-drawing and you can use it with canvas, SVG, or even positioned HTML elements; the best one that fits your project. Arbor.js simply helps you focus on the graph data and its style rather than spending time on the physics math that makes the layouts possible. [Link]

19. Gephi

Gephi is an interactive visualization and exploration platform for all kinds of networks and complex systems, dynamic and hierarchical graphs. Gephi, a graph-based visualizes and data explorer, can not only crunch large data sets and produce beautiful visualizations, but also allows you to clean and sort the data. [Link]

20. HighChartjs

High Charts JS is a charting library written in pure JavaScript, offering an easy way of adding interactive charts to your web site or web application. Highcharts JS currently supports line, spline, area, areaspline, column, bar, pie, and scatter chart types.

It works in all modern browsers including the iPhone and Internet Explorer from version 6. Setting the Highcharts configuration options requires no special programming skills. The options are given in a JavaScript object notation structure, which is basically a set of keys and values connected by colons, separated by commas and grouped by curly brackets. [Link]

21. Java Script Info VIS Toolkit

"The Java Script Info Vis Toolkit provides tools for creating Interactive Data Visualizations for the Web." This library has a number of unique styles and swish animation effects, and is free to use. [Link]

22. Axiis

Axiis is an open-source data visualization framework designed for beginner and expert developers alike. Axiis gives developers the ability to expressively define their data visualizations through concise and intuitive markup. Axiis provides pre-built visualization components as well as abstract layout patterns and rendering classes that allow you to create your own unique visualizations. Axiis was designed to be a granular framework, allowing developers to mix and match components and build complex output by compositing together basic building blocks. [Link]

23. Protovis

Protovis is a visualization toolkit for JavaScript using the canvas element. It takes a graphical approach to data visualization, composing custom views of data with simple graphical primitives like bars and dots. These primitives are called marks, and each mark encodes data visually through dynamic properties such as color and position. Although marks are simple by themselves, you can combine them in interesting ways to make rich, interactive visualizations. [Link]

24. HumbleFinance

Humble Finance is an HTML5 data visualization tool that looks and functions similar to the Flash chart in Google Finance. It makes use of the Prototype and Flotr libraries and is not limited to displaying financial data but any two 2-D data sets which share an axis. The data needs to be stored in JavaScript variables and requires three parameters to be set before running the function to create the chart. It is possible to manually select a part of the data (with a slider-like interface) and zoom to that part. This is a very useful function when working with large datasets. [Link]

25. D3.js

D3 is a small, free JavaScript library for manipulating HTML documents based on data. D3 can help you quickly visualize your data as HTML or SVG, handle interactivity, and incorporate smooth transitions and staged animations into your pages.

D3 is not a traditional visualization framework. Rather than provide a monolithic system with all the features anyone may ever need, D3 solves only the crux of the problem: efficient manipulation of documents based on data. This gives D3 extraordinary flexibility, exposing the full capabilities of underlying technologies such as CSS3, HTML5, and SVG. It avoids learning a new intermediate proprietary representation. [Link]

26. Dipity

Dipity lets you create a free digital timeline. It allows creating, sharing, embedding and collaborating on an interactive and visually attractive timelines has the ability of integrating video, audio, images, text, links, social media, location, and timestamps. [Link]

27. Kartograph

Kartograph is a framework for creating interactive maps without any mapping provider (like Google Maps). It consists of two libraries: a Python library that renders vector maps from shape files or Post GIS and converts them to SVG and a JavaScript library for turning these SVG data into interactive maps. If you already have the SVG data (for example, any drawing can be converted to SVG with Adobe Illustrator), only the JavaScript library can help too. [Link]

28. TimeFlow

TimeFlow Analytical Timeline is a visualization tool for temporal data. This tool is currently in alpha version so there is a chance of finding glitches. It provides five different displays: timeline view, calendar view, bar chart view, and table view. [Link]

29. Paper.js

Paper.js is an open-source vector graphics scripting framework that runs on top of the HTML5 Canvas. It offers a clean Scene Graph / Document Object Model and a lot of powerful functionality to create and work with vector graphics and bezier curves, all neatly wrapped up in a well-designed, consistent, and clean programming interface. Paper.js is easy to learn for beginners and has lots to master for intermediate and advanced users. Paper.js is developed by Jürg Lehni and Jonathan Puckey, and distributed under the permissive MIT License. [Link]

30. Visualize Free

Visualize Free is a free visual analysis tool based on the advanced commercial dashboard and visualization software developed by InetSoft, an innovator in business intelligence software since 1996. Visualization is the perfect technique for sifting through multi-dimensional data to spot trends and aberrations or slice and dice data with simple point-and-click methods. If you are looking for a way to visually explore and present data that standard office charting software cannot handle, Visualize Free is for you. [Link]

- See more at: http://bigdata-madesimple.com/30-simple-data-visualization-tools/#sthash.4Q8yOl3t.dpuf/ & http://bigdata-madesimple.com/30-simple-data-visualization-tools/

23. How to Begin Your Data Science Journey

1. Buy a book on modern data science; avoid statistics textbooks re-labeled as data science like plague: they will lead you to nowhere. Any public-domain stuff that's been invented 50 years ago will lead to a job that will eventually be replaced by a robot - we are working on this to make it happen. If you have an analytic background, my book is a good start. Older versions are still available for free, but the Wiley version is much more organized and easy to read, and costs less than $25. Other books can be found in the reference section below. In April, We will publish a new book data science 2.0. Initially available for free to Data Science Central members. This book will have more source code, even advanced spreadsheets, and detailed explanations on many data science concepts.

2. Read our data science cheat sheets: the version for beginners, or the more advanced version, depending on your background. Also read our resources section where you will find articles featuring plenty of useful external links about Python, machine learning, deep learning, Hadoop, R programming and more. Also check out the reference section at the bottom of this article: it offers a selection of books, training, conferences, jobs, salary surveys and other career-related stuff like job interview questions for data scientists.

3. Get data and work on real projects. Check out our project list for data science apprentices. Schools like Zipfian Academy are worth while; though it's tough to be admitted (you need a PhD).

4. Launch your career: apply for a job at AnalyticTalent.com, create your start-up (here are a few ideas for data scientists, check also this link), collect and sell data (for instance, stock market forecasts delivered via an API), become a consultant, or a digital publisher like us. And don't forget to connect with practitioners on DataScienceCentral.com - you will find people interested in your ideas, and able to help you, if you contribute intelligently.

http://www.datasciencecentral.com/profiles/blogs/4-easy-steps-to-becoming-a-data-scientist [11]

24. Can you learn data science on the job?

Since *data scientist* is a senior job title that comes with significant experience, even expertise, how can you become a data scientist fresh out of college, or from Coursera classes, or from some data science boot camp?

I believe you indeed learn data science on the job. Employers have been fooled into hiring people with R, Python, SQL, NoSQL, some outdated statistical knowledge, and little work on a small academic data project - who claim to be data scientists. There's even a joke about NoSQL: some candidates add NoSQL to their resume to tell potential employers that indeed, they don't even have SQL in their skill set. The results is a painful learning curve for the new hire once on the job, and essentially negative ROI on the high salary commanded by these individuals.

But employers could hire someone with the right background and turn him/her into a data scientist, a much better solution in my opinion. Someone with a quantitative background - maybe even a biologist - with experience working with various data sets in a professional setting could be a better fit. After all, our own intern at DSC came with a nuclear physics background fresh out of postdoc, worked on great data science projects for us, and still helps maintain one of our core systems today, even after finding a full time job with another company.

It is true that data scientists should know some stats, machine learning and algorithms, R, Python, SQL, unstructured big data, elements of real time architecture and APIs, and distributed architecture. And be familiar with some vendors such as Tableau. But these skills can sometimes be found in geographers, physicists, biologists (think about bioinformatics), epidemiologists, even some MBA's. And self-learners can catch up quickly, especially if they already know a programming language such as C, C++ or Java. But focusing only on people who call themselves data scientists is a mistake.

Think about this: before colleges offered the first MBA curriculum, there were no MBA guys. Yet there were plenty of people doing the work of an MBA. Some of them became the first ones to teach in MBA programs. And even today, plenty of people do MBA jobs (like COO, CEO, business analyst) and don't have an MBA degree. And they sometimes do it better than people with an MBA degree. The same can be said about data science.

There are of course many flavors of data scientists, and those really producing innovative science and techniques (especially in automating data processes - from defining, finding, collecting, aggregating, structuring, cleaning, summarizing, refining data, to value extraction and operationalizing the decision process), are expected to have a different background than most business or industrial data scientists. But they represent a tiny minority; they are the unicorns that erroneously too many companies are chasing-By Rahim on May 4, 2015.

25. Big data sets available for free

A few data sets are accessible from our data science apprenticeship web page.

I. Source code and data for our Big Data keyword correlation API (see also section in separate chapter, in our book)

II. Great statistical analysis: forecasting meteorite hits (see also section in separate chapter, in our book)

III. Fast clustering algorithms for massive datasets (see also section in separate chapter, in our book)

IV. 53.5 billion clicks dataset available for benchmarking and testing

V. Over 5,000,000 financial, economic and social datasets

VI.   New pattern to predict stock prices, multiplies return by factor 5 (stock market data, S&P 500; see also section in separate chapter, in our book)

VII.   3.5 billion web pages: The graph has been extracted from the Common Crawl 2012 web corpus and covers 3.5 billion web pages and 128 billion hyperlinks between these pages

VIII. Another large data set - 250 million data points: This is the full resolution GDELT event dataset running January 1, 1979 through March 31, 2013 and containing all data fields for each event record.

IX.   125 Years of Public Health Data Available for Download

X.   You can find additional data sets at the Harvard University Data Science website. I was particularly interested in their LinkedIn data set. KDNuggets is also a great resource, and for more, check out this link.

26. Cross-disciplinary data repositories, data collections and data search engines

- http://usgovxml.com
- http://aws.amazon.com/datasets
- http://databib.org
- http://datacite.org
- http://figshare.com
- http://linkeddata.org
- http://reddit.com/r/datasets
- http://thedatahub.org alias http://ckan.net
- http://quandl.com

- Social Network Analysis Interactive Dataset Library **(Social Network Datasets)**
- Datasets for Data Mining
- http://enigma.io

Single datasets and data repositories

- http://archive.ics.uci.edu/ml/
- http://crawdad.org/
- http://data.austintexas.gov
- http://data.cityofchicago.org
- http://data.govloop.com
- http://data.gov.uk/
- http://data.medicare.gov
- http://data.seattle.gov
- http://data.sfgov.org
- http://data.sunlightlabs.com
- https://datamarket.azure.com/
- http://developer.yahoo.com/geo/g...
- http://econ.worldbank.org/datasets
- http://en.wikipedia.org/wiki/Wik...
- http://factfinder.census.gov/ser...
- http://ftp.ncbi.nih.gov/
- http://gettingpastgo.socrata.com
- http://googleresearch.blogspot.c...
- http://books.google.com/ngrams/
- http://medihal.archives-ouvertes.fr
- http://public.resource.org/
- http://rechercheisidore.fr
- http://snap.stanford.edu/data/in...

- http://timetric.com/public-data/
- https://wist.echo.nasa.gov/~wist...
- http://www2.jpl.nasa.gov/srtm
- http://www.archives.gov/research...
- http://www.bls.gov/
- http://www.crunchbase.com/
- http://www.dartmouthatlas.org/
- http://www.data.gov/
- http://www.datakc.org
- http://dbpedia.org
- http://www.delicious.com/jbaldwi...
- http://www.faa.gov/data_research/
- http://www.factual.com/
- http://research.stlouisfed.org/f...
- http://www.freebase.com/
- http://www.google.com/publicdata...
- http://www.guardian.co.uk/news/d...
- http://www.infochimps.com
- http://www.kaggle.com/
- http://build.kiva.org/
- http://www.nationalarchives.gov....
- http://www.nyc.gov/html/datamine...
- http://www.ordnancesurvey.co.uk/...
- http://www.philwhln.com/how-to-g...
- http://www.imdb.com/interfaces
- http://imat-relpred.yandex.ru/en...
- http://www.dados.gov.pt/pt/catal...
- http://knoema.com

- http://daten.berlin.de/
- http://www.qunb.com
- http://databib.org/
- http://datacite.org/
- http://data.reegle.info/
- http://data.wien.gv.at/
- http://data.gov.bc.ca
- https://pslcdatashop.web.cmu.edu/ (interaction data in learning environments)
- http://www.icpsr.umich.edu/icpsrweb/CPES/ Collaborative Psychiatric Epidemiology Surveys: (A collection of three national surveys focused on each of the major ethnic groups to study psychiatric illnesses and health services use)
- http://www.dati.gov.it
- http://dati.trentino.it

http://www.datasciencecentral.com/profiles/blogs/big-data-sets-available-for-free [12]

References

(1)   http://blog.reskill.me/how-to-become-data-scientist-for-free/

(2)   How to become data scientist for free and from scratch (http://blog.mypath.io/how-to-become-data-scientist-for-free/)

(3)   http://www.datasciencecentral.com/profiles/blogs/how-to-become-a-data-scientist-for-free

(4)   http://www.datasciencecentral.com/video/video/listFeatured

(5)   http://www.analyticsvidhya.com/blog/2015/08/data-science-bootcamps-machine-learning-certifications/

(6)   https://www.kaggle.com/wiki/Tutorials

(7)   http://www.datasciencecentral.com/video/video/listFeatured

(8)   http://www.kdnuggets.com/2013/10/7-steps-learning-data-mining-data-science.html

(9)   http://insidebigdata.com/2013/09/19/getting-free-data-science-education/

(10)   http://bigdata-madesimple.com/review-of-top-10-online-data-science-courses/

(11)   http://www.datasciencecentral.com/profiles/blogs/4-easy-steps-to-becoming-a-data-scientist

(12)   http://www.datasciencecentral.com/profiles/blogs/big-data-sets-available-for-free

****

About the author

Award winning *Key Note Speaker at International Level*, Professor Ajit Kumar Roy is an acclaimed researcher and consultant. Prof. Roy obtained his M.Sc. degree in Statistics and joined Agricultural Research Service (ARS) of ICAR as a Scientist (Statistics) in 1976. In recent past he was engaged as National Consultant (Impact Assessment) for East & North Eastern States of India at National Agricultural Innovation Project (World Bank funded) of ICAR. Earlier he had served as a Consultant (Statistics) at Central Agricultural University, Agartala. He also served at CIFA, ICAR, as Principal Scientist was involved in R & D activities in ICT, Statistics, Bioinformatics and Economics. At International level he served as a Computer Specialist at SAARC Agricultural Information Centre (SAIC), Dhaka, Bangladesh for over 3years. He has successfully organized many workshops at National and International level. The author has more than 45 years of experience in Statistical Analysis, Analytics and information management. He has edited eighteen books and several conference proceedings covering the areas of statistics, bioinformatics, economics and ICT applications in aquaculture / fisheries / agriculture. His recent best-sellers are *'Applied Big Data Analytics'; 'Impact of Big Data Analytics on Business, Economy, Health Care and Society'; 'Self Learning of Bioinformatics Online'; 'Applied Bioinformatics, Statistics and Economics in Fisheries Research' and 'Applied Computational Biology and Statistics in Biotechnology and Bioinformatics'.* He now works as visiting Professor, question setter and examiner of four Indian Universities. He has vast experience in Statistical consulting, guidance and Analytics. He is widely recognized as an expert research scientist, teacher, author, hands-on leader in advanced analytics.

SELF LEARNING OF DATA SCIENCE

Back Cover

Getting started in the exciting field of data science can be a bit overwhelming. There are so many new tools, ground breaking applications and innovative ways to explore data that even experts in the field do not have it all figured out. But for budding data scientists, understanding this complex field may be just a few clicks away. The book provides a brief, understandable, user-friendly guide to all aspects of Data Science along with links to free educational sites. The author address the various skills required, the key steps in the Data Science process, software technology related to the effective practice of Data Science, and the best rising academic programs for training in the field. Data science is a hot and growing field. In this book, one will be approaching data science from scratch. The book does not presume sophisticated mathematical background. However, by its very nature the materials somewhat technical the goal is to impart a significant understanding of data science. Data Scientist' is one of the most important future STEM jobs. They need to have expertise in new technologies that help manage large datasets. These technologies and concepts include Map Reduce, NoSQL databases, MongoDB, SQL, Hadoop, Storm, etc. Focusing on Young Data Scientist inspires learners to take up Data Science giving them a head start to future careers and jobs. They can learn a lot going through the following links: 'How to Become a Data Scientist for Free', *'The Open Source Data Science Masters'*, 'Most Required Skills for a Data Scientist'. Self Learning of skill to become a good data Scientist Free Books, Videos, Blog Posts, Vodcasts, Twitter & Infografic, *YouTube, Amazon Web Services* and free *trainings* to become a Data Scientist , *Self Starter Way.* The Best Free Courses. *Most Sought After Skills Employers Are Looking For Data Scientist Positions* Data Scientist Education Requirements Data Scientist Training Programs The following comments by the industry experts may indicate the future job prospect& salary aspects of the data Scientists. Data scientist has been called *"the sexiest job of the 21st century,* "Data Scientists are the new Kings of the Silicon Valley Big Data: Career Opportunities Abound in Tech's Hottest Field. The Hottest Jobs in IT: Training tomorrow's Data Scientists. Forbes People with data analysis skills are in demand and demand is growing. By 2018 there will be a talent gap" of between 140,000-190,000 people, says the McKinsey Global Institute (in the U.S.). Winter Wyman's reported seeing a "300% increase in demand for data scientists and engineers" *'Self Learning of Data Science for Free'* is an ideal read for budding data scientists who are just getting started in the field. This book will lead you to see through the popular hype around "big data," and it will give you the knowledge and insights you need to hit the ground running in this fast-growing field., Consider this an essential reading list for the aspiring data scientist. The book will be quite useful for preparing to interview data science job candidates. The demand from business for hiring data scientists is strong and increasing. Every data science job seeking candidate should understand the fundamentals presented in this book.

www.ingramcontent.com/pod-product-compliance
Lightning Source LLC
Chambersburg PA
CBHW070327190526
45169CB00005B/1776